WICCA

MAGICAL
DEITIES

*A Guide to the Wiccan God and Goddess,
and Choosing a Deity to Work Magic With*

LISA CHAMBERLAIN

Wicca Magical Deities

Published by **Chamberlain Publications (Wicca Shorts)**

ISBN-13: 978-1-912715-13-8

Disclaimer

YOUR FREE GIFT

Thank you for adding this book to your Wiccan library! To learn more, why not join Lisa's Wiccan community and get an exclusive, free spell book?

The book is a great starting point for anyone looking to try their hand at practicing magic. The ten beginner-friendly spells can help you to create a positive atmosphere within your home, protect yourself from negativity, and attract love, health, and prosperity.

Little Book of Spells is now available to read on your laptop, phone, tablet, Kindle or Nook device!

To download, simply visit the following link:

www.wiccaliving.com/bonus

GET THREE
FREE AUDIOBOOKS
FROM LISA CHAMBERLAIN

Did you know that all of Lisa's books are available in audiobook format? Best of all, you can get **three audiobooks completely free** as part of a 30-day trial with Audible.

Wicca Starter Kit contains three of Lisa's most popular books for beginning Wiccans, all in one convenient place. It's the best and easiest way to learn more about Wicca while also taking audiobooks for a spin! Simply visit:

www.wiccaliving.com/free-wiccan-audiobooks

Alternatively, *Spellbook Starter Kit* is the ideal option for building your magical repertoire using candle and color magic, crystals and mineral stones, and magical herbs. Three spellbooks —over 150 spells—are available in one free volume, here:

www.wiccaliving.com/free-spell-audiobooks

Audible members receive free audiobooks every month, as well as exclusive discounts. It's a great way to experiment and see if audiobook learning works for you.

If you're not satisfied, you can cancel anytime within the trial period. You won't be charged, and you can still keep your books!

CONTENTS

INTRODUCTION

Compared to all other religions in the modern Western world, Wicca is highly unique in several ways. The absence of any central scripture or other holy text is one of them, as is the absence of any designated physical place to celebrate and worship.

Perhaps the biggest difference between Wicca and other religions—particularly the monotheistic "Abrahamic" religions of Judaism, Christianity, and Islam—is the belief that individuals can do more than simply pray to a supreme, all-powerful deity and hope that things will work out to their benefit. Instead, the Wiccan worldview holds that individuals can co-create with the forces of nature by linking their own personal energy with the divine through ritual and magic.

But what is "the divine" when it comes to Wicca? Who or what, exactly, do Wiccans worship? As with just about every question you might ask regarding this eclectic religion, you are likely to come across many different, and sometimes conflicting, answers. However, there are a few basic generalizations that can be accurately made, and this guide will examine these core concepts and beliefs about deity that lie at the heart of Wicca.

These core beliefs begin with the God and Goddess, who represent and rule over the male and female energies of the

Universe, and are found in all of nature. While each individual experiences these deities in their own unique way, they are at the center of this much decentralized religion—they are the focal point of rituals and holidays, and the creators and sustainers of life.

They have many individual forms, names, and representations, which can depend on the tradition one is following, as well as the time of year and even the phase of the Moon. They may play different roles in magical workings, and take turns as the more prominent focus of particular celebrations. But throughout all of their diverse roles, forms, and functions, they always remain the Goddess and the God— the ageless, timeless manifestations of the female and male forces at work in our world.

Nearly every source you read on Wicca will identify and discuss the God and Goddess to some extent. But you will also find many references to other deities as well, from a variety of ancient cultures around the world.

Gods and goddesses like Osiris and Venus predate the modern religion of Wicca by thousands of years, but have been essentially reclaimed over the past century by Wiccans (and other contemporary Pagans) who feel connected to them as a living presence in their lives.

So how do these ancient deities figure into the Wiccan cosmology? The answer here depends on whether you're asking about a traditional form of Wicca, or one of its later, more eclectic varieties.

As you may know, what we now refer to as Wicca was first popularized by an English occultist named Gerald Gardner in the mid-1900s, and then spread to North America and later to other English-speaking parts of the world. Although there were plenty of other people in that time and place who contributed ideas and inspiration to this emerging form of pagan belief and practice, it is almost always Gardner's concept of the God and Goddess that is credited as the basis that later forms of Wicca arose from.

For many practitioners who keep to the traditional duotheistic concept of Wicca, the ancient deities are simply parts, or "aspects," of the "supreme" Goddess and God and do not really have a role to play on their own.

For others, who tend to fall into the category of "eclectic" Wiccans, the inclusion of ancient deities is more polytheistic. They may have personal relationships with "patron" gods and/or goddesses, who may be part of ritual practice in their own right, in addition to the God and Goddess. They may also call on specific deities for assistance with specific magical aims, either on their own or in addition to the Wiccan deities. Indeed, the ways in which practitioners of this spiritual path identify and worship the divine are incredibly diverse.

This guide will introduce you to the Wiccan Goddess and God, as well as a number of older deities often included in contemporary Wiccan practice. You'll find some practical information on how these deities are traditionally honored by Wiccans, as well as some contextual information about the cultures they originate from.

Of course, a comprehensive book on the history and mythology of every deity ever worshipped by a Wiccan would be thousands of pages long. So for the sake of drawing some boundaries, this introductory guide focuses specifically on the ancient civilizations that have traditionally had the most influence on Wicca: the Egyptians, the Greeks and Romans, and the Celts.

We'll meet a handful of the most popular deities from each of these pantheons, and offer some ideas for beginning to connect with them if you see fit to do so. For those wanting to cultivate a relationship with any of these deities, however, this really is just a beginning. You are encouraged to study your prospective deities on a much more in-depth level as you move forward in your practice. To that end, you'll find a brief suggested reading list at the end of the guide.

First, however, let's take a closer look at the Goddess and the God, who are much revered by Wiccans around the world.

Blessed Be.

PART ONE

THE DEITIES OF WICCA

ORIGINS OF THE GODDESS AND THE GOD

Many thousands of years ago, long before any of the religions in existence today were developed, human beings experienced divinity very directly.

There was no need for churches or temples, or written texts explaining the existence and desires of an invisible, far-away, supernatural "overseer." Instead, early humans encountered the divine in their immediate surroundings. Plants, animals, rocks, mountains and streams were infused with spirit energy, as were words, songs, and stories. Nothing was "supernatural," since there was no separation between the perceived physical world and the invisible spirit world.

In some cultures, individual objects had their own distinct spirits, or "souls," while in other cultures, everything was part of the same divine source. In describing the origins of religion in human society, historians and anthropologists call the first concept "animism" and the second one "pantheism," though in practice the two worldviews would have had some overlap, as they still do today.

No one knows exactly when or how the phenomenon of individual deities first came about. We only know that as human culture evolved, so did our way of perceiving and describing this primordial spiritual energy.

The earliest deities we have records of tended to be associated with the essential components of the physical Universe—the sky, the Sun, bodies of water—and the most basic of life's needs and functions—safety, shelter, success on a hunt. The Sumerian sky god Anu is one of the earliest known examples, though there are doubtless older ones which are lost to history.

Over time, as the development of agriculture led to permanent settlements and life became more complex, the mythology of these ancient societies began to include deities who were associated with more sophisticated pursuits such as poetry, schools, and crafts—like the Roman goddess Minerva, who governed all three.

Not all deities were of equal importance or power. Some "lesser" deities guarded or inhabited specific natural places, such as a spring or a grove of trees, while other "greater" deities had the command of weather, battles, the annual harvest, and other crucial facets of life.

For the most part, deities were local—meaning they were only known to the people living in a given area. But as some societies began expanding beyond their original territories and settling in new regions—like the Romans, the Celts, and the Germanic tribes—they brought their deities with them, spreading their influence far and wide across continents. The Celtic Sun god Belenus, for instance, is one of the oldest and most widely known deities in Europe. An even older goddess,

Innana spread through space and time across Mesopotamia and into Greek civilization, where she became Aphrodite.

By the time Christianity was developing and gaining influence, there were probably tens of thousands of individual deities throughout the world, if not more. In many places, such as India, Japan, and parts of Africa and Native America, some of these deities continue to be honored today.

In most of the Western world, however, this is not the case. The rise and spread of the Judeo-Christian "God" eventually all but stamped out the ancient, "pagan" religions, particularly throughout Europe. And since the people in these regions were largely illiterate, relying on the oral tradition to pass down their beliefs and customs from one generation to the next, there's not much specific information to be found about what is now often referred to as "the Old Religion."

Nonetheless, the deities themselves never truly "died out," as the myths, epics, and other legends that kept them immortal were never completely forgotten. And small pockets of pagan worship, along with other practices that would later come to be called "Witchcraft," remained active in Europe—even through the worst of the centuries of persecution.

Furthermore, there were always at least a few curious people in each generation who studied the lore of the ancient past, keeping the flame of occult knowledge alive, and developing new ways to explore and practice what our pagan ancestors had always understood. Gerald Gardner, widely considered to be the founder of modern Wicca, was one of these people.

In the early decades of the 20th century, Gardner explored many avenues of religious mysticism and occult teachings, befriending a wide variety of influential thinkers along the way. He wound up meeting with a group of Witches practicing what

Gardner believed to be an ancient religion, which had been secretly kept alive throughout the centuries since pre-Christian times.

This group, known as the New Forest Coven, initiated Gardner and presented him with some of the spiritual teachings that he later brought to his own coven, Bricket Wood. Other occult influences, such as Freemasonry and ceremonial magic, along with Gardner's own intuitive innovations, made up the rest of the beliefs and practices that he and his initiates began to follow.

The core element of this new version of "the Old Religion" was the worship of a pagan god, usually referred to as the Horned God, and a pagan goddess, often referred to as the Great Mother.

These were believed to be ancient deities of the British Isles, who had been buried in obscurity by Christianity, but were now being pulled back into modern awareness through a duotheistic religion that later came to be called Wicca, which was rooted in gender polarity—the male and female being both opposite and equal, and present in all of nature. (Gardner's cosmology also involved a supreme higher power, which he called the "Prime Mover," but this power was beyond the ability of humans to know or understand, and therefore not of much practical concern.)

The God and Goddess, as they are referred to in their most general form, are more often described as archetypes—the masculine and feminine energies arising from the collective unconscious—than as historically known deities from a specific culture or location.

However, they can also be thought of as encompassing several individual "aspects," or "lesser" deities. Some of these aspects are also archetypes, but many are actual known deities from a variety of ancient cultures, including the Egyptians, Greeks, Romans, Celts, Norse, and Saxons. For example, the "Horned God" could have been based on a number of ancient deities, such as the Greek god Pan or the Celtic god Cernunnos (or his later English counterpart, Herne). Likewise, the "Great Mother" could be said to contain various goddesses, such as the Greek Gaia or the Egyptian Isis.

This syncretism—the combining of different deities into one—seems quite logical in Wicca, since it was also a feature of the ancient religions that Wicca draws inspiration from. Over the millennia, many thousands of deities were "absorbed" into others, including many in the ancient civilizations of Egypt and Greece, as we will see later on.

This multifaceted nature of the deities is no doubt a big factor in the rise and spread of Wicca, as it allowed for various interpretations of their identities. In fact, others in the British occult circles of the time added their own concepts to this newly emerging religious movement.

Robert Cochrane, who formed his own coven a few years after Gardner, emphasized the three-fold element of the Goddess—the Maiden, Mother, and Crone—rather than focusing mainly on the Mother aspect. And although Cochrane's form of the Craft ultimately branched away from Gardner's, the Triple Goddess is now a mainstay in most forms of Wicca.

Later, Janet and Stewart Farrar, who had been part of the Alexandrian Tradition of Wicca, incorporated the old English mythology of the Oak King and the Holly King into their practice. These were not replacements for the Goddess and God, but rather additional forms of the masculine deity—

brothers whose cyclical battles represent the dark and the light times of the year.

As Wicca spread from Europe to the Americas and beyond, more and more variations on Gardner's initial vision and concepts began to crop up. For example, some traditions might worship a Sun God rather than a Horned God, or even the Green Man, another archetype that comprises various Earth gods.

There are many different such archetypes, or "titles," found in Wicca, including the Earth Goddess, the Moon Goddess, and the Father God. These variations can be confusing to people who are new to Wicca, especially because you're likely to find at least slightly different information in every book you read, depending on the author's particular tradition (or lack thereof) and experience.

But it's important to understand that all of the different archetypes and individual deities can be thought of as being part of—or aspects of— the overall Goddess and God. There's no exclusivity or competition as there has so often been with monotheistic religions. Wiccans simply worship their deities in the forms that they connect with most on a personal level.

Those who belong to covens follow their coven's tradition regarding deities, so if the coven worships the Goddess as Selene and the God as Apollo, then these are the aspects who are honored in coven ritual. In keeping with the tradition of the earliest Wiccans, coven's names for the deities are almost always kept secret, known only to initiated members.

There is truly an incredible variety of names, titles, and visual renderings of the God and Goddess among the various traditions, covens, and individual practitioners of Wicca. No one way of approaching the worship of these deities is more correct than another—although many orthodox members of lineage-based traditions such as Gardnerian and Alexandrian Wicca might argue with that assertion.

But since Wicca, as a religion, has no official leaders or authoritative texts, there really isn't anyone who can say that another person's understanding of the Goddess and God is somehow wrong or inauthentic. If this wasn't the case, then Wicca wouldn't be the widespread and ever-growing spiritual practice that it has become.

For all the diversity within the Wiccan concept of deity, however, there are certainly some core characteristics of belief, myth and legend, and practices regarding the God and Goddess that are commonly found throughout various forms of Wicca. Let's turn now to a closer look at these multifaceted deities and their roles within the Wiccan concept of life, death, rebirth, and the perpetual cycle of Nature.

THE GOD

The God is the masculine half of the gender polarity that is at the heart of the Wiccan cosmology. As mentioned above, the Wiccan God is most often seen as the Horned God, though the Sun God is also a very common representation. While these two titles, or aspects, may be different, they are certainly linked in that they each represent a force that is essential for human survival.

The Horned God is associated with the wild animals of the Earth. He is generally depicted with either a horned headdress of some kind, or as having the head and horns of an animal—usually calling to mind the stag of the forest, or the goat of the mountain.

In Gardnerian Wicca, the Horned God was generally viewed as a male fertility god, but he is also the god of the hunt, who in prior centuries was called upon to assist the people in successfully bringing in enough meat to ensure their survival.

The Horned God is also the god of the animals themselves, representing the need for balance in terms of how humans interact with the natural world. In fact, not all horned deities of the ancient past were strictly associated with wild animals—the Egyptian Mnevis is an example of a god associated with the bull, which shows an understanding of the need to respect our domesticated animals as well.

As noted above, Wiccans might revere the Horned God as the Greek god Pan, the Celtic god Cernunnos, or the English mythological figure Herne, as well as the Welsh Bran, or other ancient horned deities.

The Sun God's role, of course, is that of providing the light and warmth necessary for plant and animal life to survive and thrive on Earth. As the Sun is the source of all life, this is the god most associated with sex and procreation, and this theme is found running throughout the Wiccan mythical cycle of the Wheel of the Year.

Both the solar holidays and the "Earth festivals" are viewed in the light of where the Sun appears to be in respect to the Earth's annual journey around it, so that the God is at his full power in the height of Summer, and then dies in the late Autumn, only to be reborn and start the cycle all over again.

The Sun God is associated with light and with fire, and has many individual aspects from various ancient pantheons, including the Celtic god Lugh, the Egyptian god Ra, and the Greek god Apollo.

THE GODDESS

As the feminine half of the Wiccan duo, the Goddess is associated both with the Earth and with the Moon. If the God is viewed as the source of life, it is the Goddess who brings life forth and sustains it.

As the Earth Mother, she tends the land—the forests, fields and crops—as well as livestock and other domesticated animals. Through her cycles of flourishing and then dying back in order to ultimately yield new life, she responds to the change of seasons in her timeless co-creation with the God.

As the Moon Goddess, she rules the night, the tides, and the flow of water around the Earth. As such, she is associated with the emotional and intuitive realms, as a counterpart to the God's masculine, action-oriented energy.

Aspects often representing the Goddess in Wiccan traditions include the Egyptian goddess Isis, the Greek goddess Diana, and the Celtic goddess Brigid, among others.

THE TRIPLE GODDESS

As mentioned above, the revering of the Triple Goddess in many, if not most forms of Wicca, is often attributed to the influence of Robert Cochrane. Cochrane was inspired by British poet and scholar Robert Graves, who wrote *The White Goddess: a Historical Grammar of Poetic Myth*, in which he proposed that a White Goddess of Birth, Love, and Death had been worshipped under many names, throughout pre-Christian Europe and the ancient Middle East.

Although historical evidence of these goddesses is not as prevalent as Graves suggested, there are a couple of known examples, such as the Celtic Brigid, who is considered a triple goddess because of her three domains: healing, poetry, and smithcraft, and the goddess Hera, who appears in Greek mythology in the guises of Girl, Woman, and Widow.

The three aspects of the Wiccan Triple Goddess, the Maiden, Mother, and Crone, represent the three phases of a woman's life in terms of physical reproduction—before, during, and after the body's ability to have a child. These names are also given to the Moon in her own cycle of waxing to Full and then waning to dark.

Some traditions emphasize the Moon connection over the life cycle by worshipping a Triple Moon Goddess, while others keep the relationship with the Earth more evenly represented by simply calling her the Triple Goddess.

But whatever she is called, each aspect—or archetype—contained within this multifaceted deity has her own particular associations, characteristics, and representative deities from pantheons around the globe.

THE MAIDEN

The Maiden represents the youthful phase of a woman's life, and the crescent-to-waxing phase of the Moon. As the Moon waxes toward Full, this is the phase associated with growth, the season of Spring, and with the characteristics of innocence, youth, independence, and self-confidence.

The Maiden's domains include art, creativity, beauty, intelligence, exploration, discovery, and self-expression. She is associated with dawn, sunrise, fresh potential, and new life.

Deities from ancient pantheons who often represent the Maiden include the Greek goddesses Artemis and Persephone, the Nordic goddess Freya, and the Celtic goddess Rhiannon.

THE MOTHER

At the Full Moon, the Goddess transforms from Maiden to Mother. This is the Summer season on Earth, when the forests become lush with life, the crops flourish, and the newborn animals grow into maturity.

The Mother is associated with midday and manifestation, as well as adulthood, responsibility, nurturing, and life in all its fullness, as she cares for all of creation.

In many Wiccan traditions, this is considered to be the most powerful of the three forms of the Goddess, as evidenced by the use of the name "Mother Goddess" in Gardner's original coven.

She is often represented by the Celtic goddesses Badb and Danu, as well as the Greek goddesses Demeter and Selene, the Roman Ceres, among others.

THE CRONE

As the Moon wanes and the Earth's bounty begins to die off in preparation for the Winter season, the Goddess is finished with her duties of motherhood, and so the Crone comes into her power.

The Crone is the wise elder form of the Goddess, who rules over transformations, visions, prophecy, guidance, aging, and endings. She is associated with dusk and the dark of night, death and rebirth, past lives, wisdom, and the furthest reaches of outer space. Although she has been a feared archetype throughout most of human history, her role is crucial, since without death there can be no new life.

The Crone is often represented by ancient goddesses of the underworld, such as the Russian Baba Yaga, the Celtic Morrigan and Cailleach Bear, and the Greek Hecate.

THE DEITIES AND THE WHEEL OF THE YEAR

As we have noted, Wicca has a fairly diverse set of practices and beliefs, which continue to evolve as more and more people are drawn to it. However, there is still a central "structure" to Wicca in the form of the Wheel of the Year—the 8 Sabbats and 13 Esbats that together create a framework for the ritual worship, mythology and lore of nature and her governing forces, represented in the form of the Goddess and the God.

The yearly cycle, which begins in Winter, follows the mythological story of the relationship between the two deities as they create life, nourish it, and then release it back into death in order to start anew.

The Sabbats include the solar holidays of the Equinoxes and Solstices, as well as the "Earth festivals," which fall on the cross-quarter days between the solar points of the wheel. These are considered the "days of power" and are occasions for ritual, celebration, and magical work.

At the Winter Solstice, the God is born to the Goddess, bringing a spark of hope in the darkest time of the year that the light of life is returning, even as the Earth is quietly resting from her labor. By the time of Imbolc she is recovering, as new life begins to stir beneath the Earth and the young God is gaining strength and power.

Next is the Spring Equinox, when the flowering of the Earth gets underway and the Goddess steps into her role as the Maiden. At Beltane, the God has reached maturity and mates with the Goddess to ensure that he will be reborn again at the start of the next New Year.

By the Summer Solstice, the Goddess is at the height of her powers in her Mother role, and the God is at his strongest, providing long days of strong light in order for all life on Earth to flourish. Their energy begins to wane then at Lammas, when the harvesting begins and the days are once again becoming noticeably shorter.

At the Autumn Equinox, the God is clearly beginning his journey back to the underworld, the growing season has come to an end, and the Goddess is preparing to step into her role as Crone. At Samhain, the harvest is complete, the God dies, and the Earth appears to go into mourning as plant life dies back and animals are preparing to hibernate.

It is here that the cycle of life and death is completed, which is why many Wiccans feel that this final point on the Wheel is the most powerful.

Throughout this cycle, the Moon is making her own journeys around the Earth, and each Full Moon, or Esbat, is a time of revering the Goddess. While the Sabbats are somewhat male-focused, determined as they are by the Sun's position in the sky, the Esbats are devoted completely to the feminine deity.

Over the course of the year, she may be honored as many different aspects, which will usually correspond with the seasons. For example, at the Full Moon in July, Wiccans may worship her as Demeter, goddess of agriculture, while in October, she may be seen as Persephone, or another goddess associated with the underworld.

Of course, the worship of the Goddess and the God isn't restricted to Sabbats and Esbats. While the Wheel of the Year provides covens, informal circles, and solitary practitioners alike with regular opportunities to honor the deities, many Wiccans with deep relationships to the Divine Masculine and Feminine will honor them every day, whether it's with a ritual candle-lighting, a brief prayer, or just a simple word of thanks for the day's blessings. But it is the Wheel that reinforces the story of the cycle of life and death, in which we all, ultimately, participate.

A FEW VARIATIONS ON TRADITIONAL WICCAN COSMOLOGY

For most Wiccans, religious practice involves the worship of a Goddess and a God more or less as described above. However, variations do exist in some traditions, and a couple of them are common enough to be worth mentioning here.

First, the archetype of "the Green Man" is often found as an addition to, or even a stand-in for, the Horned God and Sun God. The Green Man archetype is ancient and universal, found in various time periods and regions around the world, including India and the Middle East. He is widely represented in Western Europe in the form of carvings found around churches, cathedrals, and other public buildings.

Usually depicted as a human face either made up of or surrounded by leafy foliage, the Green Man is associated with the forest, vegetation, and new life, and so is often worshipped in Wiccan celebrations of Spring and Summer, and particularly at the Sabbat of Beltane.

Like the Horned God and the Sun God, he can be thought of as having different aspects, such as the Greek god Pan or the Celtic god Cernunnos, but unlike them, the Green Man has a documented, global history in his own right which predates the religion created by Gardner that came to be known as Wicca.

Another pre-existing archetypal element found in some Wiccan traditions is the mythical cycle of the Oak King and the Holly King. The origins of these figures are unknown, but they are viewed by Wiccans who revere them as dual aspects of the God—somewhat akin to the three aspects of the Goddess, but different in the sense that these two "kings" are brothers and rivals, who take turns conquering each other as the seasons move from light to dark and back to light again.

During the waxing half of the year, the Oak King is said to rule, while his brother, the Holly King, comes to defeat him for the duration of the waning half of the year. Depending on the tradition, these exchanges of power may happen either at the Solstices or the Equinoxes, but either way, their existence serves to illustrate the necessity of both light and dark, and life and death.

As mentioned above, these figures were incorporated into Wiccan practice by Janet and Stewart Farrar in the late 1970s. Their inclusion is by no means universal throughout Wicca, but over the decades they have seen an increase of attention from both Wiccans and other Neopagan practitioners. Interestingly, some practitioners equate the Oak King with the Green Man, showing that there is plenty of room for overlap and reinterpretation of deity among contemporary Wiccans.

Finally, there is one form of Wicca that practices a rather extreme departure from the traditional forms, in that the Goddess is revered above and beyond, and even to the exclusion of, the God. This is known as Dianic Wicca, or Dianic Witchcraft, and was founded in the United States in the early 1970s.

Envisioned as a safe space for women and a way of addressing the inequalities and abuses of patriarchal religions over the centuries, this tradition focuses on the feminine divine, and is called "Dianic" in honor of the Roman goddess Diana, who is widely revered as an aspect of the Goddess among practitioners.

Many Wiccans would understandably argue that this form of the Craft cannot be accurately called "Wicca," since it ignores the gender polarity and equal balance of the feminine and masculine, as represented by the Goddess and the God. Nonetheless, plenty of covens and individual practitioners focusing only on the Goddess still consider themselves to be Wiccans.

THE DEITIES
AND THE ALTAR

Many who have been following a Wiccan path for a long time will say they experience the presence of the Goddess and God throughout their daily lives, and not just during the time they dedicate to formally worshipping the deities in ritual. However, acknowledging and honoring the God and Goddess at the altar is nonetheless considered a core practice of Wicca, and is often the starting point for new Wiccans to develop their own personal connections with the deities.

Exact protocols for how the Goddess and God are represented on the altar, as well as how they are addressed, vary as widely as you would expect in a religion as diverse and dynamic as Wicca. These details are also generally either kept secret—as is the case with most covens—or held to be deeply personal by solitary practitioners. But while there is no one correct way to approach this aspect of ritual practice, there are a few basic elements of it that most Wiccans hold in common.

First, the Goddess and God are usually represented physically on the altar through the use of designated candles. Many traditions assign specific colors to each deity, so that the candle representing the God may be gold, red, or yellow, and the Goddess candle would be white, silver, or black.

Alternatively, the candles may be in a specific shape, such as a human form or another symbol representing the deity. Another possibility is to etch representative symbols into the candles with a pin or crystal point. Finally, some Wiccans use jar candles, which they can decorate with images and symbols representative of the Goddess and God, either in their general form or as individual aspects like Diana or Cernunnos.

Placement of the candles, like the placement of everything else on the altar is purposeful. Some traditions keep the two candles together at the northernmost point of the altar, while others place the Goddess candle on the left side and the God candle on the right. Many traditions also recognize the other ritual tools as being representative of either deity, and will place these tools on the altar accordingly.

For example, the God is associated with the wand and the Goddess with the cauldron. In an altar arrangement that devotes one side to each deity, the wand will be on the right side, and the cauldron on the left. Finally, additional images, such as artwork depicting the Green Man, the Triple Goddess, or specific deities from ancient pantheons may also be part of a Wiccan's altar.

Toward the beginning of ritual—after the circle is cast but before the main focal point of the particular occasion—the Goddess and God are usually verbally acknowledged as their candles are lit. This step may involve a long, formal invocation or it may just be a brief, more conversational welcoming of the deities to the ritual.

If spellwork is part of the proceedings, the God and/or Goddess, or one of their specific aspects, may be asked directly for assistance, depending on the nature of the work. The deities are thanked for their presence at the close of the ritual, and the candles may be left to burn for awhile longer or gently extinguished, depending on either the occasion itself or the tradition being followed.

REPRESENTING THE GOD AND GODDESS: A TABLE OF CORRESPONDENCES

If you're just starting out on your journey of connecting with the Goddess and the God in your own ritual practice, here are some common symbolic associations you might work with to represent them on your altar.

The God and Goddess in their most generalized forms are represented by traditional Wiccan tools, while their more specific aspects may be represented with particular crystals. Herbs, flowers, food and drink may be offered to your chosen deities as well, and a few suggestions are made here.

Remember, of course, that traditions vary widely, and that ultimately what feels right to you is what matters the most, so be creative and enjoy the process of discovery!

Deity	Altar Tools	Candle Colors	Images & Symbols	Offerings
The God	censer, wand, athame, boline	Gold, red, orange, yellow, green	Crescent moon on top of circle	bread, basil, clover, pine needles, fruit
The Horned God	bloodstone, green tourmaline, tiger's eye	green, gold	horns, spears, swords, arrows	cheese, pine cones, nettles
The Sun God	sunstone, citrine, carnelian	red, orange, yellow	sun, flames	sunflower seeds and petals

Deity	Altar Tools	Candle Colors	Images & Symbols	Offerings
The Goddess	cup, pentacle, bell, cauldron	black, white, silver, green	circle flanked by two crescent moons	white or purple flowers, chamomile, hibiscus, olive oil
The Maiden	clear quartz, rose quartz, amethyst	white, pink	waxing moon, owl, deer	pink flowers, white wine
The Mother	bloodstone, rose quartz, garnet	red	full moon, cauldron	roses, milk, honey
The Chrone	jet, onyx, obsidian	black	waning moon, lantern, key	red wine, apples

THE NEXT STEP

Now that we've introduced the Wiccan Goddess and God in their major, overarching forms, we'll meet several of the ancient deities that many Wiccans have incorporated into their personal practice, whether strictly as aspects of the God and Goddess, or as full deities in their own right. We'll also discuss ways in which you might consider approaching these goddesses and gods as you work toward developing your own personal pantheon.

Once again, keep in mind that these are select groups of deities from each pantheon, based on their popularity among Wiccans, as well as the amount of existing knowledge about their origins and roles within the ancient societies that gave rise to them. There are many more for you to explore on your own if you wish to, and after reading through this guide, you'll have a solid grounding to start your quest from.

PART TWO

THE ANCIENT
PANTHEONS

RECONNECTING WITH OUR PAGAN PAST

As we saw in Part One, the occultists of the mid-20th century who gave rise to Wicca and other forms of contemporary Witchcraft were reaching back to what they envisioned as "the Old Religion." However, little historical information was available for reconstructing the actual pre-Christian religion that was theorized to have existed throughout Europe.

Therefore, these spiritual pioneers drew from the occult knowledge of prior centuries and from their own intuitive gleanings to create new belief systems that echoed what was lost when Christianity all but eradicated pagan cultures.

Gardner was drawn to specifically English archetypes as he sought a way to give specific form to the divine male and female energies he sensed to be existing outside of and in spite of the dominant Judeo-Christian worldview. Others conceived of the Goddess and God in somewhat different ways, adding to and revising Gardner's concepts as they saw fit.

This process of reinvention ultimately incorporated several deities who had been worshipped in ancient times. These came most often from the religions of the Egyptians, the Greeks, and the Celts, although other ancient deities, particularly from the

Hindu and Norse pantheons, have also become increasingly popular with Wiccans.

They may be incorporated as "lesser aspects" of the Goddess and God, in keeping with traditional Wiccan duotheism, or they may be worked with as separate, distinct identities, by more eclectic polytheistic practitioners.

These deities may be adopted as "patron" gods or goddesses, with whom the Witch maintains an ongoing relationship, or may be honored at particular points along the Wheel of the Year. They may also be appealed to for specific types of magic with which they are associated.

It may seem odd to some to "borrow" a deity from another religion to worship in a Wiccan context. However, as we will see in the following overviews of the ancient cultures they are borrowed from, the adoption of deities from another religion isn't at all a new practice.

Throughout the history of human society, people have merged and adopted deities from those they came into contact with, blending aspects of their own religion with that of the new one. This can be seen today in Ireland and Latin America, for example, where pagan gods have been made into Christian saints.

In fact, many Wiccans and other pagans take the perspective that all deities, and even all religions, come from the same original source. The remains of nearly identical prehistoric tombs in parts of Europe, Asia, and the Middle East, at a time when travel between these faraway places would have been quite minimal, is one phenomenon that points to this theory. Another is the similarity of imagery found in prehistoric art from around the globe, including handprints, faces, and spiral patterns in the same distinctive styles.

Furthermore, the cosmologies and myths of many ancient civilizations have common themes, such as deities of the sky, the earth, and the underworld, and myths about creation and destruction. If you study these and other similarities from various ancient and prehistoric cultures, it's not so hard to see the possibility that everyone is ultimately drawing from the same well of divine inspiration, and interpreting the energy of that source through their own unique perspectives.

So how do Wiccans choose deities to work with in their practice? There are a number of ways these relationships might come about.

Those who join an existing coven will obviously be following the deities the coven worships in its rituals. However, for solitary Wiccans, and even for coven members who might also maintain a personal practice, the choices are really wide open.

While the most common sources are the pantheons of ancient Egyptian, Greek, Roman, and Celtic civilizations, Wiccans might work with deities from any pantheon, from anywhere around the globe, including India, Africa, Asia, the Americas, and even the indigenous cultures of Australia and New Zealand. Many people choose to work only with deities from their own hereditary cultural heritage, as a way of linking with their ancestors from past millennia. Others are drawn to deities with no connection to their own family or ethnic history.

As Wicca has become increasingly widespread, there has been much discussion about "appropriation" of deities from existing cultures. As a result, some Wiccans choose to work only with deities from "lost" religions, such as that of the ancient Egyptians, Celts, or Norse. Deities from Native America or India might be considered to be an overreach, since they are still worshipped by their own people today, even if it's to a lesser extent than it was a few hundred years ago. Ultimately, however, these decisions—like so much else in Wicca—are up to the individual.

If you're new to Wicca, or not-so-new but still looking to expand your practice to incorporate one or more new deities, there are a few ways to go about your search. You might, as others have done, research the ancient culture(s) of the parts of the world your own ancestors came from. Or, perhaps there's a particular region and/or culture that has always intrigued you for some reason you can't quite put a finger on—if so, start looking at their history, mythology, and pantheon to see what intuitive connections you might discover.

Many Wiccans will say that their deities found them, not the other way around, so be sure to listen to your inner knowing as you ponder the question of who you might link up with in the astral realm.

You can also ask the Goddess and the God to make themselves known to you in the aspects that are most appropriate for your own practice. This might occur via a dream, or some other sign or signal. When an answer becomes apparent, read all you can on the deity (or deities) in question, so you'll have a clearer sense of who you're seeking to forge a relationship with.

Of course, that advice goes for every deity you're considering, no matter how you arrived at his or her name as a possible patron. The more you know about the gods and goddesses you seek to work with, the more authentic and astounding your connection with them has the potential to be. And while you're certain to find plenty of information on the most well-known deities from the ancient world in Wiccan and other pagan sources—especially pertaining to magical associations—it's very worthwhile to seek out non-religious texts as well.

Read historical information about the people and the culture the deities originated from, as well as the original myths they appear in. Get a well-rounded education in your deities of choice, rather than simply adopting the perspective of one or a few Wiccan practitioners. After all, the relationship between Wiccans and their deities is intensely personal and unique to each individual.

Another thing to keep in mind as you contemplate your options is the idea of "pairing" gods and goddesses who would not have been well matched in their original cultures. Those who follow a duotheistic Wiccan path will often worship a specific male and female aspect of the God and Goddess as personal patron deities.

Some have discovered that choosing from two different pantheons—for example, the Greek Artemis as the Goddess and the Celtic Lugh as the God—doesn't result in a very harmonious energy. Furthermore, two deities from the same pantheon may not appear to be a good match if they were on opposing sides of a conflict in the culture's mythology.

On the other hand, there are those who experience no difficulty whatsoever in a "mix and match" approach to deity worship. Again, this is a personal choice that must take your own understanding of deity, along with your intuition, into account. No one else can choose for you—nor should anyone try to.

Also, know that you may or may not stay aligned with the same deities throughout your life. Many Wiccans find that new deities come into their lives as their circumstances change and their sense of spirituality evolves. So you're not necessarily making a lifelong commitment when you choose a deity (or when a deity chooses you). Think of it more as a decision to engage in a serious process of discovery, and then see where it leads.

The following pages provide an overview of the major ancient civilizations whose deities and religious practices have had the most influence on contemporary Wicca: the Egyptians, the Greeks and Romans, and the Celts.

While other pantheons have also become quite popular in recent decades, such as the Norse, Hindu, and several Native American deities, it is this classic "trio" that inspired so many of the occult scholars whose work eventually gave rise to Wicca, and so it seems the most fitting place to start.

Each pantheon discussion is followed by a table of correspondences with suggestions for representing and honoring the deities at your altar, as well as the chief magical purposes you might ask for their assistance with. So let's meet the ancestors with the closest ties to the Wiccan vision of "the Old Religion."

THE EGYPTIAN PANTHEON

A QUICK HISTORY OF THE EGYPTIANS

What we think of as "ancient" Egyptian civilization is indeed one of the oldest, and longest-lasting, civilizations in human history.

However, the Egyptian pantheon is not a fixed collection of deities who all came into being more or less at the same time. In fact, over the course of more than 5,000 years, Egypt's cultural and political situation experienced several different shifts, which gave rise to different deities over time.

In the earliest days, each region within what became known as Egypt had its own local deities. As these regions began to merge, so did their cosmologies. Generally speaking, the conquerors of an area would absorb the local religion of the area into their own, so that deities with similar functions would be merged together under the name of the conquerors' deity.

However, in other cases, two or more deities might be contained within a larger deity—somewhat like the Wiccan God and Goddess with their varying archetypal aspects. One significant example is the war and protection goddess Bast, who was eventually paired with another somewhat similar goddess, Wadjet, to become Wadjet-Bast.

As Egypt became a more united civilization, around 3,000 B.C., several of these deities rose to a much more universal status. These include Isis, Osiris, Horus, and Thoth. However, the popularity and importance of any given deity still fluctuated to some degree during different time periods.

Similarly, the associations of many deities, their visual representations, and the details of the mythology surrounding them often morphed and changed over the course of the region's history. For example, there are a few versions of the god Horus, two of which are known as Horus the Elder and Horus the Younger. Each has different parentage, and different outcomes in what is essentially the same central mythological story.

Toward the end of Egypt's ancient era, when the land came under Greek rule, some of the Egyptian deities became absorbed into the Greek cosmology as well. Isis was one of these, and her influence was so strong that she even had worshippers throughout the Roman Empire by the time Christianity was beginning its conquest of Europe.

So as you can see, the pantheon of Egypt is incredibly complex, providing a rich diversity of deities and their associations with the natural world as well as the intricacies of human life.

COSMOLOGY AND BELIEFS

At the heart of the Egyptian concept of the Universe was a constant tension between chaos and order. The ideal, clearly, was order, a state of being which the Egyptians called Ma'at, and which also encompassed the ideals of truth and justice. It was the responsibility of both human beings and the gods to maintain this order, which was believed to be at constant risk of dissolving into disorder, and so required a conscious commitment to living in cooperation with one another.

The deities, being in control of the forces of nature, needed to participate in this balance in order for human life to thrive. Egyptian religion existed, in large part, to keep the gods functioning in harmony with the natural order and to prevent the Universe from descending into chaos.

The chief intermediary between the gods and the people was the King of Egypt, or Pharaoh. Through his divine power, he had to perform rituals and make offerings to the gods so that order would prevail.

Of course, he had help, in the form of priests and temples throughout the kingdom. The temples served not only as places of worship, but as libraries where ritual instructions were kept—both on papyrus scrolls and in the form of engravings.

Religion wasn't strictly a state affair, however. Individuals could also make offerings to the deities and ask for assistance with their own personal obstacles and struggles. They might appeal to the patron deity of their region, or to a deity associated with their particular need.

For example, someone living in Thebes in the earlier part of the Egyptian era might make offerings to the patron god Montu for general well-being, while a woman wanting assistance with matters of beauty might appeal to the widely-worshipped goddess Hathor.

MAGIC

Ancient Egyptian religion has been of particular interest to Western occultists over the centuries, perhaps because of its emphasis on magic, or what the Egyptians called "heka."

Heka was the natural force through which the Universe had been created, through which the gods manifested their desires, and which could be used by humans to overcome obstacles and influence events in their favor. Like contemporary Wiccan magic, it was seen as a way of affecting outcomes through indirect means.

The rituals that took place in the temples were considered to be a form of magic, but ordinary individuals could also manipulate heka through rituals of their own, as well as the use of sympathetic magic, spells and incantations, and magical objects, such as protective amulets made from precious stones and inscribed with magical symbols.

Written instructions for such rituals and spells—what might be called ancient Egyptian "grimoires"—were part of the temple libraries, and eventually made their way through the general population, where magic was a common practice.

MYTHOLOGY

As is true of all ancient pantheons, a number of Egyptian myths serve to illustrate the characteristics of the deities and their functions in both the natural world and in the affairs of human life.

Of course, as cultures and geographical boundaries in ancient Egypt shifted and blended over time, so did the details of these stories, so that many myths can be found to have different, and even conflicting versions. Nonetheless, most myths retain a central core that can be identified through several versions of a tale.

This is the case with perhaps the most important myth of Egyptian civilization—the story of Isis, Osiris, and Horus—a trio of the most widely known deities in the pantheon. Again, the tale has varying details and outcomes, depending on the region and time period of the teller, but the basic gist of it is worth recounting here.

Isis and Osiris are twins, born to the Earth god Geb and the sky goddess Nut. But they are also recognized as husband and wife, which is fairly common in ancient mythologies, as the gods and goddesses inhabit a vastly different "reality" than do human beings.

As Geb's eldest son, Osiris inherits his father's kingdom, and becomes the first Pharaoh. But another sibling in this family, Set, is jealous and murders Osiris in order to gain the throne.

The body of Osiris is—depending on the version of the story—hidden and/or dismembered and scattered throughout the country. Isis, however, manages to find the body and magically resurrect it long enough to conceive a child with Osiris.

She gives birth to Horus, who grows up and defeats Set, becoming the new Pharaoh. Osiris, meanwhile, has become the ruler of the underworld, while Isis has forged her reputation as a goddess of motherhood and magic, among other things.

The story is seen as a rationalization for the connection between the Pharaoh and the heavens, with Set associated with chaos and disorder, and Osiris and Horus representing the rightful rulers of Egypt.

Next, we'll take a look at some of the variations of this tale as we explore some of the principal deities in the Egyptian pantheon. This group includes Isis, Osiris, and Horus, as well as the well-known god Thoth, who plays a minor but important role in the story of Isis and Osiris. We'll also meet the goddess Bast, who is not involved in this central myth, but who nonetheless was widely revered in ancient Egypt and still has followers today, many of whom identify as Wiccans.

As you read on, keep in mind that there is always more to know than can possibly fit into this brief overview guide, so be sure to explore further into any deities who catch your interest!

BAST

Originally worshipped as a goddess of warfare in the earlier years of Egypt's long history, Bast was first represented as a lioness, in the delta region of the Nile River. Once the cultures of Lower and Upper Egypt united, Bast was one of many deities whose position shifted, and she ultimately became a goddess of protection, represented in the form of a cat.

Though her status diminished over time, the cat association was no small thing, as cats were highly revered in Egypt. Hundreds of thousands of mummified cats were discovered at her temple, and her annual festival was indeed a highly festive event, featuring singing, dancing, and the playing of flutes and rattles.

Her name was later altered to Bastet, which in the Egyptian language signaled her descent from her earlier power, and most scholars now refer to her with this name. However, among her contemporary worshippers, including many Wiccans, she continues to be known as Bast, and her significance continues in spite of the changing tides of Egyptian history.

Bast's protective and cat-like nature is shown in the mythology that surrounds her. As the daughter of the Sun god Ra, she was said to ride with him each day as he pulled the Sun across the sky, but she became even more crucial at night while her father slept, standing guard against his enemy, the serpent Apep.

Ultimately, Bast was able to kill the serpent using her magical all-seeing eye. The victory ensured that fertility and abundance would continue to bless the inhabitants of the Nile delta, as the Sun's existence was no longer threatened.

Many Wiccans hold Bast dear in large part due to her status as the patron goddess of cats, who are, of course, the animals most commonly associated with Witches. However, Bast is also considered a fertility goddess and an ideal model of motherhood, as cats are known to be protective of and nurturing to their young.

Their skill in stalking mice and other vermin make Bast particularly known as a protector against disease as well as evil spirits. But cats also love to play, which is why she is also a goddess of joy, music, and dancing. Bast is additionally associated with perfume, healing ointments, music and magic.

Throughout most of ancient Egyptian civilization, she was regarded as a Sun goddess, but by the time Greek culture had merged with that of the Egyptians, she had become associated with the Moon.

To work with Bast, you can create an altar to her with images of cats and/or lions, especially images showing a mother cat with her kittens. She is also traditionally represented with carvings or other images of baskets and sistrums (the music-making rattles of ancient Egypt.) Suggested offerings include milk, honey and other sweet foods, and perfumes.

Call on Bast for assistance with conception, childbirth, and motherhood, as well as the prevention of illness and protection during travel. Place an amulet depicting the all-seeing eye—

called an *utchat*—over your door for protection against thieves and other ill-intentioned visitors.

If singing, dancing, and/or chanting appeal to you as means of magic, Bast is the perfect goddess to invoke while doing so. You can also keep her playful-yet-protective energy with you by carrying cat's eye or tiger's eye stones in your pocket.

Other magical goals ideal for assistance from Bast include help for animals, overcoming hostile opposition, and finding more humor and joy in daily life.

OSIRIS

One of the oldest and most widely revered deities of Egypt, Osiris was particularly well-known and worshipped at the sacred city of Abydos, just a few miles west of the Nile. The story of Osiris' death and resurrection is central to the ancient Egyptians' concepts of life, death, the afterlife, and the importance of order in the world.

Known as a kind and compassionate ruler before his demise at the hands of his brother Set, Osiris was believed to have brought civilization to Egypt by teaching his people to grow crops, follow laws, and worship the deities appropriately. As a deity associated with disorder, Set could not bear the adoration and success of Osiris and therefore killed him by tricking him into a large, beautiful chest, locking him in it, and throwing the chest into the Nile, where it floated out to sea.

In one version of the central myth, Isis travels the world until she finds the chest, opens it, and magically resurrects Osiris for long enough to conceive Horus. Afterward, the body is embalmed by the god Anubis, which initiates the tradition of mummification. In another version, the chest washes ashore and becomes part of a tree trunk before Isis discovers it.

In some variations, Set hacks the body to pieces after he discovers what Isis has done, causing her to rescue her husband's remains a second time, while in others, the dismemberment occurs first. All of the versions, however, end with Osiris as the ruler of the dead, where he awaits the newly-deceased and helps them adjust to their new existence in the underworld.

The cyclical flooding of the Nile was associated with Osiris' death and resurrection in a couple of ways. In one legend, the flooding is the result of the tears of the mourning Isis after he is murdered. But others viewed the return of the much-needed waters as symbolic of the resurrected Osiris, and therefore associated him with abundance and life as well as with death and the underworld. He was even associated by some with the harvest, with the dismembering of his body representing the process of cutting and threshing grain.

This dual association of life and death can be compared to the Wiccan mythology of the God's cyclical death and rebirth, which makes Osiris a compelling aspect for many Wiccans.

He can be called upon in magic to assist with difficult transitions and endings, as well as new beginnings. He provides help in seeing the positive aspects of an apparently negative situation, and in harmonizing relationships where separation has occurred due to the harboring of resentment, envy, and other negative feelings. Any work aimed at regeneration, peace, or restoring order to chaos can also fall under his domain.

To represent Osiris on your altar, you can use depictions of the Pharaoh holding a crook and flail—the traditional tools of the shepherd—and/or the colors black and green, to represent the soil and rebirth.

ISIS

Known throughout the Western world as a mother goddess and a queen of magic, Isis is probably the most famous deity of ancient Egypt. She originated as a funerary goddess, and unlike most Egyptian deities, she was worshipped almost universally throughout the land. She was so popular, in fact, that her cult survived centuries into the Christianization of the Roman Empire, in the form of her last official temple on the Egyptian island of Philae.

Isis' name translates to "throne" in the ancient Egyptian language, and she is often represented as a woman with a throne headdress, which symbolizes her enormous power and status. She traditionally holds the *ankh* symbol in one hand, which represents eternal life.

Like her twin Osiris, Isis is associated with both life and death, as it was she who resurrected her dead husband in order to bring forth new life in the form of their son, Horus. Her passion and her magical skills are illustrated by the central myth, in which she goes to the ends of the Earth to find the lost body of Osiris, brings him momentarily back to life, and ultimately avenges his murder by raising the child who will grow up to depose the murderer, Set, from the throne of Egypt.

Her tears of grief over the loss of Osiris are said by some to be the source of the cyclical flood waters of the Nile. In another story, Isis uses her sorcery to gain power over the Sun god Ra by creating a serpent. The serpent bites Ra, and Isis promises to heal him only if he will tell her his secret name.

Isis is also strongly associated with motherhood, since she became the mother of the Pharaoh once Horus took the throne, and a mother of Egypt in her devoted assistance to Osiris as he taught the people the ways of civilization. She is also a protector of children, as she had to guard Horus against his evil uncle Set from the moment Horus was born, as well as a protector of the dead. She represented love and faithfulness, spirituality and dreams, and inner wisdom and destiny.

It was the 19th-century British Order of the Golden Dawn that first revived the revering of Isis, and her universality as a goddess may have been what drew Gerald Gardner and other early Wiccans to include her in their worship.

While Isis began in ancient times as a solar goddess, she was eventually transformed into a goddess of the Moon during the period of Greek rule in Egypt, which is closer parallel to the way goddesses are perceived in Wicca. In many traditions, Isis is considered a triple goddess, embodying birth, life, and death.

Her magical connections are many, and include, of course, magic itself. You can call upon Isis to aid in any creative magical endeavor, especially those involving fertility and growth, but also healing, and protection.

To connect with her in a dream state, place rose petals under your pillow before going to sleep. To honor her in prayer, wear white and/or silver, and carry amethyst or bloodstone charged on an altar devoted to Isis. Candles, incense—especially myrrh and jasmine, and flowers are appropriate offerings, along with milk and honey.

A strong relationship with Isis can bestow many blessings and protective interventions, when necessary, in your life.

HORUS

Another of the oldest and most important deities of the pantheon, Horus existed in several distinctly different forms over the long time span of ancient Egyptian civilization, and eventually became a patron god on a national level.

He was known as a sky god, and a god of war, hunting, and protection, and was particularly important to the belief in the link between the Pharaoh and the gods, as he was the one to defeat the evil Set and restore order to the land from the King's throne. Over the centuries, the pharaohs would eventually claim direct lineage from Horus, strengthening their image as divine rulers.

Horus is the son of Isis and Osiris, who battles with Set—his father's murderer—in many different stories, and protects Egypt from him according to his mother's wishes. Ultimately, Horus and Set come before the Sun god Ra to make their cases for the throne, and Ra rules in Horus' favor. The various myths and legends around this epic conflict contributed to Horus' exalted status as a hero.

Horus was originally a falcon god, flying through the sky on his hunt, and at festivals honoring him, a live falcon was crowned to represent his sovereignty. He has also been depicted as an infant sitting on a lotus petal, since his childhood was intricately linked with Isis' mother-protector role in the central myth.

As a sky god, Horus was seen to rule both the Sun and the Moon. His powerful eyes reflected these dual domains, with one eye associated with the Moon, and the other with the Sun. (Which eye is which depends on whether you're looking at an image of Horus or visualizing his actual perspective.)

The long-revered symbol known as the Eye of Horus is usually associated with the Moon, while the Eye of Ra symbolizes the Sun. However, the Eye of Horus is more familiar in the present day, perhaps because of Horus' dominion over both celestial bodies.

The eye of Horus is a particularly beloved symbol for many Wiccans, who appreciate the powerful protection it conveys, and its association with reincarnation, a central tenet of Wiccan belief.

In a magical context, Horus is the son of the great magician Isis, and so his energy is considered to be especially strong, as well as forceful and even aggressive, given his status as a warrior and king. Though Wiccans reject the use of magic for negative and even overtly manipulative purposes, the assistance of Horus can be channeled for positive intentions, particularly when aimed at problem-solving and helping those in need.

You might call on Horus for assistance in navigating an interpersonal conflict, or in "hunting" for needed sustenance. Drawing or painting the Eye of Horus symbol is believed to attract protective energy and good health—in fact, this is a popular design on clothing as well as a common tattoo for Wiccans and other Pagans.

Represent him at your altar with images of falcons, hawks, or other birds of prey. Offerings to Horus traditionally include raw meat to honor the falcon aspect, but vegetarians can use bread as an appropriate alternative. Iron and symbols of weaponry honor the warrior aspect, as well.

THOTH

Although Thoth's rise to prominence occurred relatively late in the history of ancient Egypt, he is one of the earliest Egyptian deities in the cosmology. Thoth is said to be "self-created" as opposed to being born to another deity, and is credited with a wide variety of contributions to civilization, including writing, medicine, and magic.

His chief temple was located in Khmun (which was later named Hermopolis by the Greeks, who associated him with Hermes), but Thoth had numerous shrines throughout Egypt.

He is often represented visually with the head of either an ibis—a sacred bird in Egypt—or a baboon, a clever animal associated with Thoth in legends. As a lunar deity, he may appear wearing a crescent on his head, and is often seen with a scroll and a reed pen to signify his association with writing, language, and communication.

Thoth was considered by many to be the heart and tongue of the Sun god Ra, speaking on Ra's behalf and therefore wielding enormous influence in the creation of the world. He and his wife, the goddess Ma'at (who personified the Egyptian concept of order, truth, and justice and was also self-created) stood on either side of Ra in his boat as he pulled the Sun across the sky each day.

In one legend, Thoth is actually responsible for the creation of Ra, by laying an egg in his form as an ibis, from which the Sun hatched. Thoth also has a role in some versions of the central myth of Isis and Osiris, providing Isis with the magical incantations necessary to resurrect Osiris from the dead. He is also said to have helped Osiris bring civilization to the people by providing instruction in arts and science. Thoth is credited with writing thousands of books, including several texts on hermetic wisdom and magical arts.

It is this last connection that made Thoth so significant to the British occultists of the late 19th and early 20th centuries, and what inspired Aleister Crowley to name his Tarot deck and accompanying manual *The Book of Thoth*. (As for the "original" Book of Thoth, there are many ancient Egyptian manuscripts to which this title is given.)

Indeed, as the god of wisdom, knowledge, learning, and magic, Thoth is an obvious choice for any Wiccan or other Witch to respect and work with. Many call upon him for assistance in workings related to acquiring new knowledge or clarity, communicating effectively, mediating disputes, healing, and gaining a higher level of mastery of the magical arts.

To honor Thoth, you can place images on your altar of ibis or other long-legged wading birds, baboons, or scrolls of parchment. You can also revive the ancient practice of leaving offerings of writing tools, such as inks, pens, pencils, etc. (Modern versions work just fine, though if you can find some old-fashioned or even hand-made writing tools, all the better!)

Lunar-shaped candles, water, beer, and bread also make for fine offerings to Thoth. You could also use books about ancient Egyptian religion, since he is credited with inventing it!

WORKING WITH EGYPTIAN DEITIES: A TABLE OF CORRESPONDENCES

Deity	Candle Colors	Images & Symbols	Offerings	Types of Magic
Bast	red	cats, tiger's eye, baskets, sistrum	sweet foods, perfumes	protection, motherhood, joy
Osiris	black, green	pharaoh, crook and flail	bread, incense	regeneration, peace, restoring order
Isis	black, blue	moon, hawk, amethyst, bloodstone	milk, honey, flowers, myrrh	magical power, fertility, growth, healing, protection
Horus	black, gold	falcon, hawk	raw meat, bread	hunting, justice, triumph
Toth	black, white	ibis, baboon, parchment scroll	water, beer, bread	knowledge, communication, magical skill

THE GREEK AND ROMAN PANTHEONS

A QUICK HISTORY OF THE GREEK AND ROMANS

If you've had any experience with the Classical era, whether in history, art, literature, or science, you'll know that the civilizations of ancient Greece and Rome were very much intertwined for several centuries. The term "Greco-Roman" is often applied to this time period and to the integrated cultures of the two peoples.

The Greeks and the Romans were neighbors for centuries before the Roman invasions that ultimately conquered Greece, but their cultures were initially very different from each other. And although Greece was technically the conquered society, it was the Romans who ended up adapting to Greek culture, rather than the other way around.

This is particularly evident in the arena of religion, where just about every Roman deity has a Greek counterpart, which is why these two pantheons are often grouped together as they are in this guide.

Later on, we'll meet three deities from each civilization, but first let's take a closer look at the Greeks, who so inspired their Roman neighbors, along with much of the rest of the world.

THE ANCIENT GREEKS

It has been said that no ancient civilization has had more influence on our way of life in the Western world than that of the Greeks, who are credited with inventing a range of cultural ideas and art forms, including philosophy, geometry, and comedic theater, as well as the foundations of democracy.

They also left a lasting legacy in the form of their gods and goddesses, whose colorful characters and stories have appeared in Western art and literature for centuries.

The Greek pantheon is quite populous, with well over a dozen major deities and many more minor ones. Different locales had their own specific patron deities, but most Greeks worshipped the same major gods and goddesses, give or take a few.

The principal deities included those who resided on Mount Olympus, the tallest mountain in Greece, and are often referred to as the Olympians. These include Zeus, the ruler of all other deities, Aphrodite, the goddess of love and beauty, and Apollo, the god of music, poetry, and the Sun, among other associations.

Another main group is the primordial deities—the gods and goddesses of the Earth and sky, seas and mountains, the underworld, and even aspects of the human experience like aging and sleep. Gaia, the Earth and mother goddess, is chief among this group, along with Chronos, the god of time, and Nyx, the goddess of night.

There are also dozens of "lesser gods," many of whom were very popular, despite ranking low in the hierarchy of the pantheon. Pan, the goat-legged Earth and fertility god, is one of these, as is Heracles, a protector god, and the 9 Muses of creativity.

GREEK MYTHOLOGY AND MAGIC

The Greeks believed their deities to have the same appearance, and even the same foibles of character as human beings, meaning they were prone to jealousy, selfishness, and rash behavior. This is illustrated in many of the myths, which often include negative consequences of excess, such as when Narcissus falls in love with his own reflection in a pool and, unable to tear himself away, wastes away to nothing staring at it.

Although they were immortal, goddesses and gods were not all-powerful, as the Greeks believed in Fate as the ultimate power in the lives of humans and deities alike. They were also not wholly separate from the realm of humans—many stories show gods and goddesses interfering in the daily lives of mortals and even mating with them.

These unions produced demi gods and goddesses, who, along with many nature spirits, contribute to the high degree of complexity in the Greek pantheon. The nature spirits, collectively known as nymphs, have parallels in the belief systems of some Wiccans and other Witches today.

Another aspect of ancient Greek religion that has had obvious influence on modern Wicca is the association of many goddesses with the Moon—namely Selene, Artemis, and Hecate, with Selene usually seen as the actual personification of the Moon. (This contrasts with the cosmology of ancient Egypt, where the Moon deities tended to be male).

As for magic, there is plenty of evidence that it was widely practiced in Greece. In fact, the English word "magic" comes originally from the Greek "magikos." Magical practices occurred in both religious and non-religious contexts, and included spells for love and healing, ritual chants, and invocations of deities.

It's interesting to note that much of the written evidence of magic dates from after the Greeks conquered Egypt, and suggests significant Egyptian influence—this is yet another example of how Wicca's adoption of beliefs and practices from other cultures is nothing new. But if the Greeks borrowed from the Egyptians, they themselves were also very heavily borrowed from by the Romans, as we will see next.

THE ROMANS

The ancient people now known as the Romans originally belonged to an Italic tribe called "the Latins" who established several settlements along the central western coast of the Italian peninsula. The city of Rome grew from a small village into a teeming metropolis over the span of a few centuries, and developed an increasingly civilized and complex culture—in no small part thanks to its neighbors, particularly the Etruscans to the north and the Greeks to the south.

But the Romans were clearly not content to just keep to their original territory, and over the centuries they extended the borders of their Empire to include places as far away as southern Scotland, northern Africa, and Turkey. They spread their culture and religion throughout the lands they occupied, but when it came to Greece, which predated Rome by about 1000 years, they really were no match.

With a much richer culture, Greece was widely influential in the Mediterranean region, and so it made more sense to adopt many of their myths, ideas, and even deities. However, they used their own names for the deities, turning Artemis into Diana, for example, Dionysus into Bacchus, and Aphrodite into Venus. They also changed details of the stories to suit their own culture and worldview—because, for all the similarities they may seem to have, the Romans were not much like the Greeks at all.

Greek culture was sophisticated, filled with literature, art, philosophy, and the celebration of ideas. The Greeks enjoyed the finer things in life, and valued individualism, revering the heroic deeds and cultural contributions of great soldiers, athletes, and thinkers. The Romans, by contrast, were strict and stern, emphasizing a sense of duty and obedience, working hard for the greater good of society and downplaying individual desires.

Roman culture was largely agrarian and concerned with the acquisition of more land, so the bravery of warriors was an ideal standard to live up to, as they valued actions over ideas. But they didn't celebrate individual soldiers so much as they prized the accomplishments of Romans as a people.

For the Greeks, the motivation to accomplish great things was to be recognized and remembered by their society. For the

Romans, it was the reward in the afterlife that mattered— they believed that they could be elevated to god-like status if they led exemplary lives of good and heroic deeds.

These differences can be seen in Roman mythology, where the gods and goddesses are far more practical and functional than their emotionally unpredictable Greek counterparts. They were also more subdued and composed than the Greek deities, and conformed more to the militaristic, patriarchal framework of Roman society.

For example, Mars, the most prominent god of war, represented the order and stability achieved by military victory, whereas Ares, his Greek equivalent, was more associated with chaos and destabilization. And the Greek warrior goddess Athena, once she became Minerva, was given the more tame associations of arts, sports, and wise strategy, reflecting the Roman ideal of war as a strictly masculine activity.

The myths themselves focus more on the founding of Rome and its politics and wars, rather than on the personalities of its deities. Perhaps this comparative lack of flair is why Greek mythology is so much more well-known, and why the Romans themselves were so keen to adopt it! Whatever the case, far less is known about Roman deities and myths in the period before Greek influence took root than after.

ROMAN RELIGION AND MAGIC

The Roman religion, in keeping with its culture, was one of serious devotion to its native deities. And unlike ancient Greece, where government and religion were separate realms, Roman religion was very much intertwined with politics. In fact, politicians often rose to power by becoming priests.

Government decisions, particularly those related to war, were never undertaken without consulting the appropriate deities first. This was done through various methods of divination, including dream interpretation, observing animal behavior (in particular the flight patterns of birds), and "scrying" from the entrails of animal sacrifices.

Deities were honored at all public events, and the calendar year was full of festivals devoted to specific gods and goddesses. Furthermore, every type of vocation had a patron deity, and every household had its own spirits and ancestors, who were honored with daily rituals.

Magic was also widely practiced in Rome, even though it was officially frowned upon by the government and many attempts were made to prevent its use, including laws against even possessing magical knowledge.

Despite the threat of persecution, however, magic was a thriving business, with plenty of professional magicians available to meet the needs of the average citizen. People sought magical intervention in many areas of life, including love and luck, gambling, healing, and protection from evil spirits.

However, there was no "harm to none" philosophy in Roman magic—people also paid magicians to work curses against their enemies. These workings usually involved amulets, sympathetic cord magic, and/or the inscription of spells onto lead tablets, which tended to be addressed to specific deities, and were often buried in graveyards.

Ultimately, the vast reach of the Roman Empire at the height of its power had much to do with the stamping out of pagan practices throughout Europe.

It was the Emperor Constantine who first converted to Christianity, paving the way for it to become the official religion of the Empire by the year 400 AD. But as we have already seen, the pagan deities of the ancient world never truly and completely died out, as they have inhabited the imaginations of countless writers, artists, and occult scholars for centuries.

Today, many reconstructionist pagan groups are even making efforts to revive religious practices of ancient Greece and Rome, among other pre-Christian civilizations. And of course, many Wiccans work with these two pantheons.

Next, we'll meet a handful of the most widely worshipped deities. These include the Greek Earth goddess Gaia, the nature god Pan, and the mysterious Hecate, "queen of Witches", as well as the Roman love goddess Venus, Diana, goddess of the hunt, and Bacchus, god of wine and revelry. These are, of course, just a few brief introductions, so don't hesitate to explore these and other deities from the Greek and Roman pantheons!

PAN

Of all the widely-known Greek gods and goddesses, Pan has had perhaps the most influence on the Wiccan concept of the male deity. He is an ancient horned god, half-man and half-goat, who is associated with fertility and the forest. But he is also a god of mischief and mayhem, representing the unpredictability of both human nature and of the wild.

Pan lived on the outskirts of the civilized world of the Greek deities, preferring the freedom of the wilderness, but he still enjoyed a good party and was often in lustful pursuit of female company. He is also associated with music—in fact, he gave the pan flute its name—and was often referred to as "the god heard, but not seen," as though he might be looking in on a celebration from the edges of his wild kingdom, playing music for the benefit of the people but choosing to stay hidden.

Greek mythology has conflicting stories about Pan's origins, but he is believed to be older than the more famous Olympian deities. However, most of what is known about Pan comes from folklore rather than the classical mythology itself.

Pan was thought to assist Greek armies in fending off invaders, by creating so much noise the soldiers would think they were under attack and started killing each other by accident. In fact, Pan is where the word "panic" comes from. He was said to induce a different kind of panic on dancers at parties, who would find themselves dancing wildly and nearly uncontrollably once Pan descended upon the festivities with his music.

Worship of Pan was generally a boisterous, all-night outdoor affair with fine food, drink, and sex, with the distinct sound of pan pipes playing in the background. Revelers often experienced visions of the god during these rituals.

Wiccans and other Pagans revere Pan for his association with both wild goats and domesticated flocks, shepherd, hunters, nature spirits, ecstatic music and fertility. Because of this last connection, he is often invoked at Beltane.

As a sexual god, it's important to note that Pan is all about lust, rather than committed love and partnership. Therefore, don't appeal to him for help in attracting a lasting relationship!

Pan is much more an embodiment of the untamed passions that all humans are capable of letting loose, which explains why he's the inspiration for renditions of the Devil card in many Tarot decks, including the classic Rider-Waite. Some Wiccans ask Pan for help increasing their musical skills.

To honor Pan, it's traditional to approach him by making noise of some kind—most commonly by clapping and singing or chanting, or playing musical instruments. It is said that Pan doesn't like to be startled, and so it's best to "warn" him that you're about to address him.

Offerings of wine are appropriate, as are honey cakes for the nymphs—or nature spirits—that often accompany him. On your altar, you can include images of wild goats and/or other forest creatures, or even a pan flute. Of course, since Pan is the god of the wild, you may find it more appropriate to commune with him outdoors, perhaps in a wooded area.

GAIA

Over the past few decades, the popularity of the Earth goddess Gaia has spread widely throughout the Pagan world. For Wiccans, she is a primordial archetype of the Mother Goddess, giving birth to and nurturing all of creation.

Her name comes from the Greek word for "land," which is "ge," and the root of the English words "geology," "geography" and even "geometry," which initially referred to the measurement of land.

For many in the environmental movement, Gaia has come to symbolize the planet Earth itself, and she is often represented in contemporary art as a pregnant woman, with the globe painted onto her protruding belly. Ancient Greek artists portrayed her as a voluptuous woman stretched out on the Earth, or rising up out of it.

Gaia is believed to be the Greek version of an older, neolithic-era mother goddess. In the Greek cosmology, Gaia was born of Chaos, the primordial force that preceded creation.

In turn, Gaia brought forth the sky, the sea, and the mountains. She mated with Uranus, the sky god, and gave birth to the Titans—the first divine rulers of the world. She also gave birth to many creatures and sea deities, and her grandchildren became the most well-known gods and goddesses of the pantheon—the Olympians.

Gaia was also a goddess of prophecy, and one mythical story has her predicting the overthrow of her son Chronos by one of his own children, which then comes to pass despite Cronos' efforts to prevent it.

There is plenty of evidence to suggest that the famous ancient shrine in Greece known as the oracle at Delphi, where priestesses would speak prophecies that came from the god Apollo, was originally dedicated to Gaia. The oracular power of the site was believed to be directly connected to her Earth energy.

For this reason, some Wiccans call on Gaia to assist in various forms of divination. She is also invoked for magic involving transformation of all kinds, and bringing creative projects to fruition, along with abundance and prosperity.

Fertility is another key association, along with any work related to the turning of the seasons, healing through herbs and other natural remedies, and—perhaps most crucially in this modern age—healing the environment. Perhaps more than any other deity, Gaia teaches the necessity of balance, as well as gratitude. For this reason, she is often worshipped at Autumn sabbats, but any point along the Wheel of the Year is appropriate for honoring the Earth.

An altar devoted to Gaia might have any kind of stones or crystals, as well as soil, plants, and/or images of trees and other greenery. Suitable offerings include harvested fruits, vegetables, and grains. However, it's also an excellent idea to be outdoors, either sitting or standing with bare feet on the ground.

One magical tradition involving Gaia is to gather a few pinches of soil from the Earth and carry them with you in a cloth sachet or a sealed container. This is especially useful when you're struggling to keep a promise or a resolution—either to yourself or someone else. When you feel tempted to stray, release a little of the soil back to the Earth to keep you grounded and connected to your highest self.

HECATE

Believed to have originated outside of Greece—possibly Egypt or southwest Asia—before being assimilated into the Greek culture, Hecate was initially a mother goddess, associated with childbirth and the female reproductive process.

Her name has been given several possible meanings. "Hecate" is said to be a feminine form of "Hekatos," which was a rarely used name for Apollo. It is also said to mean "most shining one," which would correlate with portrayals of her wearing a starry headdress and holding a torch.

However, she later became associated with witchcraft, sorcery, ghosts, and the spirit world. Some argue that this was due to the advent of male-dominated societies becoming the norm, with a fear of women's power. We will probably never know, but we do have an additional meaning for Hecate's name, which is "she who works her will." As such, she is a beloved patron goddess of many Wiccans and other magic-practicing Pagans.

In Greek mythology, Hecate tends to be seen as a powerful outsider. She is adopted by the Olympians, but never lives among them. And yet, in the earlier myths, Zeus grants her dominion over the Earth, the seas, and even the heavens, and she appears to be his equal.

Later myths show her as Zeus' daughter and associate her with the Underworld. In one story, she is sent there to rescue Persephone who has been captured by Hades. Hades is reluctant to give Persephone up, so an arrangement is made to let her spend half of the year with the living and the other half in the Underworld with the dead. Hecate becomes Persephone's chaperone as she moves between the worlds. As time went on, Hecate became increasingly depicted as a frightening hag, associated with the waning Moon and restless spirits, ultimately becoming known as the Goddess of the Dead.

Crossroads were traditionally associated with Hecate, most likely because of the crossroads that the newly dead would encounter in the Underworld. She could manifest as a black dog, considered a guardian symbol of both houses of the living and of the entrance to the realm of Hades.

She is often portrayed holding a snake—another symbol of the dead—and wearing a belt with the keys to the spirit world. She may be accompanied by a three-headed dog, or have the "triple head" of a dog, snake, and lion. Compared to the earlier representations of her with the torch and headdress of stars, it's clear that her darker aspects became more prominent as time went on!

Wiccans revere Hecate's title of "Queen of the Witches," and many see her as an example of a triple goddess, even though she doesn't quite fit the description in the classic sense. She is mostly a crone goddess, due to her associations with magic and death, and is called upon for help with transformational magic during the "dark" time of the year, beginning at Samhain. Some traditions worship Hecate and the Celtic goddess Brighid as alternating deities of darkness and light, with Hecate ruling over the waning half of the year, and Brighid ruling the waxing half—something like a feminine version of the Oak King and Holly King.

To honor Hecate, leave her offerings of raw eggs, cheese, or garlic at a crossroads, or decorate your altar with images of snakes, black dogs, owls or ravens.

VENUS

Unlike many Roman deities who were Greek in origin and simply adopted by the Romans, Venus was native to Rome, and was actually considered to be the divine mother goddess in the mythology of the foundation of the Roman people.

In keeping with the functional nature of the pantheon, she was associated with gardens and vegetation in general, including blossoms—the delightful Spring promise of new life to come. In this spirit, she was also a goddess of sensual love, which is reflected in her name—"venus" is a Latin word relating to seductive beauty, charm, and mating.

As the Roman and Greek civilizations began to merge, Venus took on the characteristics and mythology of Aphrodite, who was also a goddess of love and beauty. And although she has other domains as well, including prosperity and victory in war, she has remained throughout time as a symbol of the undeniable power of the feminine.

In keeping with her multiple roles, there were several forms, or aspects, Venus could take in Roman mythology. As the divine ancestor of the Roman people, her mother goddess aspect was known as Venus Genetrix, while the warrior goddess was Venus Victrix. As a goddess of fortune, she was Venus Felix, and, in a seeming contradiction, she was also associated with the virtue of female chastity, known as Venus Verticordia.

This last role is likely a holdover from her pre-Aphrodite identity, since she later became known as a seductress who took many lovers, including the native Roman god of fire, Vulcan, and Mars, the god of war. Mars, of course, is regarded even today as the male counterpart to Venus' quintessential female energy.

In visual representations, Venus is almost always depicted as a beautiful and voluptuous young woman, and is symbolized by roses, doves, trees, pine cones, and wild berries.

For Wiccans, Venus is predominately associated with the domain of romantic love, though many seek her assistance in matters of friendship and family, as well as gardening and prosperity. She is typically honored during one or more of the Spring sabbats—Imbolc, the Vernal Equinox, and Beltane—in keeping with her roles as goddess of new growth and of sexual passion.

Call on Venus for all desires related to love and romance. If you're looking for a new relationship, place bay leaves under your pillow to encourage prophetic love dreams. If you're already romantically involved, bay leaf tea can re-energize the passion in your relationship. If you need an extra boost of feminine energy to balance out strong masculine forces in your life, gather several flowers and pine cones—the traditional symbols of Venus—and place them around your environment where you will see them constantly.

To commune with her in nature, be on the lookout for large stones situated next to a tall tree—Venus is said to always be present in these places. To honor Venus at your altar, use pine cones, Spring blossoms, and/or an image of her from ancient

Greco-Roman art. Offerings can include slices of "exotic" fruits like pineapple and mango, bay leaves, and roses.

BACCHUS

Bacchus, the god most known for his association with wine, was not native to the Romans, but wholly imported from the Greeks. While he was somewhat identified with the older Latin god Liber—also associated with wine and revelry—the mythology surrounding Bacchus seems to be entirely Greek in origin, with names and some details changed to fit better into Roman culture.

In Greece, he was Dionysus, and although he has plenty of Wiccan followers under this name, he is also widely known in his Roman form throughout Wiccan and other Pagan communities. This may be due in part to Bacchus' prominence in the Roman pantheon once he was brought in—he was considered one of their Council of Gods, known as the "Dii Consentes." However, his roles as the god of wine, revelry, hilarity and good cheer may also have something to do with it.

In some ways, Bacchus could almost be likened to the Greek Pan, in that he brought a high degree of festivity to ancient worship. In a culture as serious and order-driven as ancient Rome, Bacchus would have offered a delightful and welcome contrast.

His devotees tended to get wildly drunk and rebellious, to the extent that the government of Rome eventually banned his festivals. In fact, to this day the word "bacchanalia" is used to refer to festive, drunken, raucous parties. There is also a tie-in with sexual excess, and some people equate "bacchanal" with "orgy," though this is likely misrepresenting history, or at least stretching the truth. The Latin word "orgia" actually referred to secret rites attended only by women, and such rituals did exist to honor Bacchus.

Of the festivals attended by both sexes, much was written about "indecent" sexual behavior, but these reports were from conservative Roman statesmen who didn't care for this "wild Greek element" in the Roman culture, and historians believe they are exaggerated or even completely made up. Nonetheless, the association with uninhibited sexuality stuck.

In mythology, Bacchus is actually something of a romantic, rescuing the goddess Ariana (the Roman name for the Greek Ariadne) from the sea and marrying her. Their relationship was among the most romantic of the ancient pantheons, and he remained faithful to her until her death.

Bacchus is also a shapeshifter, able to transform into a lion or a bull when need be, and is sometimes portrayed in a chariot being pulled by lions. He was credited with the discovery of grapes and their wine-making potential, and sacrifices to him always involved goats and/or swines, since both animals were destructive to grapes and could potentially ruin a harvest.

Wiccans who work with Bacchus often honor him at Beltane, in association with sex and general revelry, but may also incorporate him into sabbats at the end of Summer, to coincide with the grape harvest.

Spiritually, Bacchus represents the need to "let loose" on occasion, and he may be called upon to help you release constrictions in any area of your life or your personality. Just as wine can help people say and do things they would be too inhibited to otherwise, the energy of Bacchus can help break up stagnant, restrictive energy. To honor him at your altar, wine and grapes are the obvious choices for both offerings and imagery.

DIANA

Like Venus, Diana was also a native Roman deity, who only later became associated with a Greek equivalent—the goddess Artemis.

Initially a hunting goddess associated with the forest and wild animals, Diana eventually became closely associated with the Moon. Her name has been translated as "heavenly" or "divine," due to its roots in an ancient Indo-European word for "sky."

Diana is widely revered in several Wiccan and other Pagan traditions, particularly those who focus primarily (or exclusively) on the divine feminine. In fact, she's the deity from whom Dianic Wicca takes its name. Even so, Diana is also honored and worked with by Wiccans who follow the traditional concept of gender polarity.

As goddess of the hunt, Diana was most famously worshipped in a sacred oak grove near Lake Nemi, which was in the countryside outside of Rome, surrounded by woodlands. Her festival was called the Nemoralia and was sacred to women, who underwent elaborate cleansing and beautifying rituals in order to prepare to visit her temple.

In Roman mythology, Diana was regarded as a "virginal" goddess who vowed never to marry, and her attitude toward males can be seen in one story in particular.

Bathing in a stream while on a hunt, Diana is spotted by a young man named Actaeon, who feels compelled to approach her and praise her for her beauty. In response, Diana turns him into a stag, after which he is attacked by his own hunting dogs. This fierce independence from male energy is likely the inspiration for those Wiccans and Pagans who practice Dianic forms of worship.

As a lunar deity, Diana became associated with women and childbirth, and in the old Italian religion of Stregheria, she was the Queen of the Witches, meaning that she ruled over the wise women and healers of the land.

These two associations have led many Wiccans to see her as an ultimate triple goddess. She is the Maiden in her huntress role, the Mother in her role as protector of women in childbirth, and the Crone in her role as leader of wise women.

In ancient Roman art, she is usually depicted as a young beautiful hunter with her bow and arrow, often surrounded by wild animals. It's interesting to note that she was both hunter and friend to animals, with a reputation for being able to talk to and influence their behavior.

In magic, Diana is often called upon for assistance in matters of fertility, protection, and abundance. If you want to honor her at your altar, include images symbolic to either or both of her major roles—bow and arrows, forest animals and vegetation, and Moon and water symbols. She can also be communed with in an oak grove, or in other quiet wooded places.

Try following an ancient Roman tradition by writing your petition to Diana on a strip of cloth or ribbon and tie it to a tree branch. You can leave offerings to her, such as blueberries, eggs, or white wine, in a forest or at a crossroads. Finally, the

Full Moon is an excellent time to approach Diana, particularly in the Summer and Autumn months.

WORKING WITH GREEK AND ROMAN DEITIES: A TABLE OF CORRESPONDENCES

Deity	Candle Colors	Images & Symbols	Offerings	Types of Magic
Pan	purple, brown, green	goat, pan pipes, caves, mountain forests	wine, honey cakes	lust, passion, music
Gaia	green, blue, brown	serpent, bees, harvested crops, green calcite, amber, honeysuckle	honey, barley, sage or rose incense	business, abundance, childbirth, divination, marriage
Hecate	black, orange	snake, black dog, raven	eggs, cheese, garlic	justice, knowledge, magical power, protection, psychic ability
Venus	pink, white	spring flowers, pine cones	exotic fruits, bay leaves, roses	love, lust, friendship, family
Bacchus	red, purple	chalice, lion, bull	wine, grapes	fertility, celebration
Diana	silver, white	bow and arrow, forest animals, vegetation	blueberries, eggs, white wine	courage, liberation, magical power, success, wisdom

THE CELTIC
PANTHEON

A QUICK HISTORY
OF THE CELTS

Although the influence of the Celts and their pantheon on contemporary Wicca is very significant, theirs is perhaps the most mysterious of the ancient civilizations covered in this guide.

This is largely due to the fact that they kept almost no written records, but it's also because, unlike other ancient peoples, they had no central government or homeland—instead, they were mostly independent tribes who migrated from Central Europe to some of the furthest reaches of the continent over the span of several centuries.

They left very little specific information about their religious practices, and most of what is known about their deities comes from the lore of Ireland and Wales, which is by no means comprehensive.

Nonetheless, the colorful tales in the surviving mythology, along with rich traditions of nature worship and magic found within these particular lands, have inspired many Wiccans—so much so that Celtic Wicca is now a widely practiced form in its own right.

HISTORY AND IDENTITY

The earliest verifiable evidence of Celtic settlements dates back to around 1200 BC, in what is now Austria, but as a people they are believed to be several centuries older.

By the year 100 BC, the Celts had spread throughout Western Europe, especially into Northern Italy, Spain, Portugal, France, and the British Isles, and they also moved eastward as far as Turkey. The bulk of the Celtic territory on the European continent was known in ancient times as Gaul, though other groups inhabited this region as well.

The Celts had remarkable influence in many aspects of pre-Christian Western European culture, including languages, the arts, technology, religion, and education. However, the Celts weren't interested in building an empire—their motivations for migrating into new lands were rooted in trade and an expanding population, rather than extending a centralized power.

Therefore, they didn't attempt to conquer the cultures of the lands they settled, but rather integrated their own ways with those of the people they encountered. This means that there was no "standard" Celtic culture—for example, the Celts living in Northern Italy would have been quite different from those living along the North Atlantic coastline.

To make matters more complicated, the Celts didn't believe in writing down their body of knowledge, as they thought it better to safeguard their cultural and historical heritage by committing it to memory. This means that most of what is known of the Celts comes to us solely through archeological remains and the writing of outside observers, including Greek and Roman writers and later, Christian monks. (The Celts were literate and made use of both Greek and Roman alphabets, but only for mundane purposes.)

Ultimately, the Roman Empire came to control the Celtic lands, and the rise of Christianity that followed, combined with the invasions of the barbarian tribes that led to the Dark Ages, all but wiped out their culture, mythology, and religion.

However, there were a few isolated areas where the Celts were mostly left alone by both the Romans and the barbarians. These mainly include the lands of the "Insular Celts"—Ireland, Scotland, and Wales—and so it is these particular areas that give us most of our knowledge of the Celtic pantheon and accompanying mythology, thanks largely to Christian monks who recorded as much as they could of this slowly vanishing world.

However, historians of this part of the world are quick to point out that these islands were inhabited for thousands of years before the Celts arrived, and so there's no telling how much of the culture and mythology was adopted, rather than brought, by the Celts.

For one thing, two of the most widely-known "Celtic" deities—Brighid and the Dagda—are actually remnants of an older, Neolithic society who were absorbed into the Celtic pantheon. This is hardly unusual, as we've seen similar blending in the pantheons of Egypt, Greece, and Rome, but it's a useful example of how the Celtic "identity" is not as straightforward as many New Age Celtic enthusiasts might think.

RELIGION, CULTURE, AND MYTH

For all the diversity of the greater Celtic world, however, there were a few common cultural characteristics to be found among its people. Perhaps the most important aspect for Wiccans is the emphasis on nature in Celtic religion.

Rather than constructing elaborate temples for the worship of their deities, they held the land itself to be sacred, and honored many local nature gods and goddesses at holy shrines near rivers, springs, lakes, groves of trees, and natural rock formations.

They also held plant and animal life to be of utmost importance, as can be seen in their use of tree names for the letters in the Ogham alphabet and the special status given to particular animals like the stag, the boar, the salmon, and the crow.

Like the Romans, the Celts believed in reading omens in the behavior of birds and the entrails of sacrificial animals, and would consult such oracles before undertaking any important activity. And like many pagan societies, they marked important points on the Sun's journey around the Earth with ritual ceremonies—particularly at Imbolc, Beltane, Lughnasa, and Samhain, which became the four "Earth festivals" of the Wiccan Wheel of the Year.

Another element of Celtic society that has fascinated Wiccans and other contemporary Pagans is the role of the Druids, the "learned class" of priests, philosophers, poets and healers who were responsible for keeping the knowledge of the people intact.

They were the Celts' teachers, who instructed their students in medicine, science, mathematics, geography, astronomy, philosophy, and law, as well as religion. Druids served as judges in disputes between individual tribal members and entire tribes, and as advisors to kings and warriors. Many of them were also highly skilled in magic, particularly in the areas of divination and prophecy.

The importance of the Druids to the Celtic world can be seen in their appearance in many Irish and Welsh myths, where their powers are sometimes elevated to shapeshifting and transforming other humans into animals. In some of the most famous stories, Druids even live with and advise key figures like Conchobar, the King of Ulster, and Finn, the hunter/warrior/hero god.

Throughout the diverse lands they inhabited, the Celts worshipped an enormous number of individual deities. Inscriptions of more than three hundred have been found across Europe, and many were equated by the Romans with their own gods and goddesses.

The majority of Celtic deities were local to a particular area or tribe, though a handful could be said to be pan-Celtic, existing in different forms in different places but with related names and characteristics. Lugh, Belenus, and Cernunnos are three examples of pan-Celtic gods.

Many deities were associated with aspects of the natural world, such as Manannan mac Lir, god of the sea, while others presided over aspects of human civilization, like the healer Dian Cecht and the blacksmith Goibhniu.

However, the Celtic deities are not as easily categorized as those in other ancient pantheons. There was more than one deity for some roles, such as healing, and many deities had a wide range of functions and associations, which could include both human circumstances and the natural world.

As mentioned earlier, what we know of the Celtic pantheon comes mostly from the Irish and Scottish mythological tradition, followed by mythology from Wales, and to some extent Cornwall and Brittany. It's worth remembering that these ancient stories were recorded by monks, who often doctored the tales with their own Christian slant, so that many of the characters are referred to as "kings" and "heroes" who had supernatural powers, rather than as deities.

Nonetheless, these sources are full of colorful tales of deities and mortals, battles and magic, earthly life and the Otherworld. The Irish myths revolve around the Tuatha de Danann, the "divine race" to which the Sun god Lugh and the triple goddess Brighid, among many others, belong. The Welsh myths inhabit a somewhat different world, with divine characters of their own, including the horse goddess Rhiannon, the giant king Bran, and the shapeshifting goddess Ceridwen.

Next, we'll meet a handful of the Celtic deities most commonly worshipped by Wiccans, including Lugh, Brighid, and Rhiannon, as well as the Dagda, a father god of the Irish pantheon, and Cernunnos, the ancient horned god who has inspired generations of modern-day Pagans. As always, make a point of exploring these and other Celtic deities further, since this brief introduction is only the beginning!

THE DAGDA

If there were to be a Celtic equivalent to Zeus or Jupiter, widely considered the "father gods" of the Greeks and Romans, it would have to be the Dagda. Though he likely originated in a pre-Celtic society in central Europe, he eventually became an important figure in Irish mythology as the leader of the Tuatha de Danann.

Usually portrayed as a giant, the Dagda was associated with abundance, fertility, and protection, and his name is said to translate to "the good god." He was also revered by Druid priests as a god of knowledge who granted wisdom to those who were willing to learn.

The Dagda is the father of many important deities in the Irish pantheon, including Diancecht, the god of healing, Aengus, the god of love, and Brighid, the goddess of healing, poetry, and smithcraft.

The Dagda was said to protect the crops of the land as well as the tribe. He was a fearsome warrior with a giant club that could both kill—up to nine men in one blow—and restore life to the fallen in battle. For this he was also known as a god of life and death.

The Dagda possessed other magical items as well, including a bottomless cauldron of that never ran out of food, called the

Undry, which had a ladle large enough for two men to lie in it. He also had a lavishly decorated harp made of living oak, known as "the Four Angled Music," that he would play to put the seasons back in order. For this, he was considered by some to be a god of time and the Earth.

Portrayals of the Dagda usually show him with his harp slung over his shoulder and his club being dragged behind him. As a giant with a reputation for insatiability when it came to food and pleasure, he is sometimes represented in a comical light, wearing clothing that is far too small for him and appearing oafish, but this is thought to be the work of the Christian attempt to delegitimize the pagan deities of the Celtic lands.

He may also be seen with two pigs, which were also among his magical possessions. It was said that one pig was always growing while the other was always roasting.

Wiccans who work with the Dagda revere his connection to magic, to abundance, and to the seasons. He may be called upon for help with matters of protection, weather, healing, prosperity, and resolving disputes. He is also revered by those who work with music or are pursuing education.

If you wish to connect with the Dagda, light a candle for him at an altar decorated with leaves and branches from an oak tree (or any tree), images of fields of bountiful crops, harps, and/or items to represent the four seasons. Listen to music that features the harp, or celebrate a hearty feast in his honor.

Because of his power over the seasons, any Earth festival is appropriate for worshipping the Dagda, but his association with life and death make Samhain a particularly good choice.

BRIGHID

Daughter of the Dagda, Brighid is another member of the Tuatha de Danann who evolved from a pre-Celtic society, and is believed to have originally been a Sun deity. There are actually several variations of her name, including Brigit, Bride, and Brigh (pronounced "Bree"), but all are usually translated as "exalted one."

Revered in Ireland, Scotland, and Wales under various names, Brighid is considered a "triple goddess" in the sense that she has three primary associations—healing, smithcraft, and poetry. Some believe that she was actually three "sister goddesses," all named Brighid, who were later merged into one, but her worshippers usually hold that these seemingly separate deities were always simply aspects of the complex, three-fold goddess that is Brighid.

Patron deity of poets, healers, and magicians, Brighid was so popular in Ireland that the Christian Church chose to make her a saint rather than try to suppress her worship.

In fact, the Catholic clergy even transformed a shrine to Brighid into a convent. The shrine, in the Irish county of Kildare, had been tended for centuries by nineteen priestesses who kept an eternal flame burning in her honor, and this tradition remained in place until the 13th century, when the patriarchal forces of the Church finally could no longer tolerate such veneration of the divine feminine.

Nonetheless, the Celtic world never completely gave up their relationship with Brighid—whether she's thought of as a goddess, a saint, or some combination of the two, she is still honored at holy wells throughout Ireland, Scotland, and Wales as she was for millennia. People would toss gold or brass rings into the wells as offerings, and you're still likely to find coins in these holy waters. It's also still a common practice to offer prayers to tie ribbons or strips of cloth to trees in the vicinity.

In Irish mythology, Brighid was said to have been born at sunrise, with a tower of flame bursting from her head and reaching all the way to heaven. Brighid possessed the cauldron of inspiration, from which poets and bards could draw in order to compose their works.

This creative force also extended to magic, crafting in general, and to childbirth, as Brighid was known to watch over women in labor. She was a mother herself, and one story has it that at the death of her son, Ruadan, she began the tradition of keening—weeping and shrieking—as a grieving ritual.

Brighid has widespread appeal to Wiccans as a "classic" triple goddess, even though some see her strictly as the maiden aspect while others see her as the mother. Her association with magic and smithcraft can also suggest a crone element, for those who wish to work with her in a triple goddess context.

She can be called upon to assist with a number of magical purposes, particularly those associated with inspiration, healing, and manifestation of creative intentions. She is most associated with the festival of Imbolc—so much so that it is commonly called "Brighid's Day" in Ireland and by Celtic Wiccans.

To honor Brighid, try writing a poem to her and/or leave offerings at a natural spring or at a place where three streams come together. Appropriate altar imagery includes flames, water, the hearth, metal items to represent smithcraft, and flowers—especially dandelions and trilliums. Corn, oats, garden sage, and pumpkin seeds make suitable offerings.

LUGH

Although he is a prominent figure in Irish mythology, Lugh was worshipped widely throughout the Celtic world, as is seen in place names and inscriptions throughout Europe. Like other pan-Celtic deities, he is known by different names in different places—he was called Lugos in Gaul, and Lleu in Wales.

Primarily a Sun god, his name has been translated as "shine" or "shining one," but at least one myth also has him associated with grain. The Celtic festival of Lughnasa, celebrated at the beginning of August, reinforces this dual association as it relates to both the sun and the harvest.

But Lugh was not just a god of nature—he was a very well-rounded deity associated with many skills and talents, from building and metal work to poetry and music, and was also known as a great warrior and magician.

Lugh was such an important god to the Celts that he was mentioned in writings by Julius Caesar, who likened him to the Roman god Mercury. Lugh's festival was adopted into the Roman calendar, renamed for Augustus, and held to be the most important holiday in the Gaulish Celtic lands.

At least fourteen cities in Europe were named for him, including Leiden in the Netherlands, Loudoun in Scotland, Lugones in Spain, and Lyon in France, which originally called

Lugdunum, meaning "Lugh's fort," and was believed to be the center of Gaulish worship devoted to Lugh.

It is also believed that many sacred sites dedicated to him were later occupied by churches. He is often depicted as a fair young man holding a spear.

Lugh's many talents are the focus of at least one famous myth, in which he gains entry to the hall where the high kings of Ireland meet. He is told that he cannot enter, because they will only admit one person who can play the harp, one who is skilled in smithing, one who is an excellent builder, etc., and that they already have guests who fill those roles.

Lugh states other talents that he possesses, such as storytelling, sorcery, and healing, and is told that they already have those roles filled as well. Finally, Lugh asks if they have anyone who is skilled in all of these areas at once, and this is what gets him in the door.

In a Welsh myth, Lugh is killed by his wife and her lover, which results in perpetual Winter until he is restored through magic, which brings the return of Spring and begins the cycle of the seasons.

Lugh's association with the Sun and his role in the turning of the seasons makes him a highly appropriate god for Wiccans to connect to. His many talents also make him a very versatile deity who can be called upon for assistance with magic, healing, the arts, building and crafting, and prevailing in any number of difficult situations.

Like Brighid, Lugh is traditionally honored with his very own holiday on the Wheel of the Year, which is also known to Wiccans as Lammas and August Eve. It's Irish custom to light a bonfire and dance around it at this feast.

To honor Lugh, decorate your altar with images of the Sun and/or anything representative of one of his many associations. Leave offerings of bread or grains.

RHIANNON

Possibly one of the most beloved deities among today's Wiccans and other Pagans, Rhiannon has been called the "Divine Queen of Faeries" and is a goddess of the Moon. Welsh in origin, she is associated with both fertility and the Otherworld, embodying the life-and-death cycle that the Moon represents, and was said to have been born at the first moonrise.

Rhiannon is famously associated with her white horse, which has led some scholars to associate her with the Gallo-Roman goddess Epona. She was also said to have the command of singing birds who could both sing mortals to sleep and wake spirits from the dead.

Although she has much power and skill, Rhiannon also faces steep obstacles and strife in the stories that surround her, making her very relatable to those who worship her.

As is the case with many Celtic deities, most of what is known about Rhiannon comes from the mythology which was not recorded until many centuries after the stories originated. However, we do know that horses were widely used in the Celtic world, so to be connected with this very important animal was definitely a sign of regal divinity.

Several giant prehistoric carvings of white horses have been found in England, created by digging deep enough into the grassland to expose the white chalk bed underneath. Until a century or so ago, festivals were held in which the people would scour the figures clean in honor of the sacred horse. Some scholars believe these festivals honored Rhiannon, specifically.

In the stories, Rhiannon appears as a golden goddess riding her white mare, and is too fast for her suitor, Pwyll, to catch up with her until he finally calls to her to stop. They marry, and her divine status means that Pwyll becomes King.

Later, when their infant son is kidnapped, Rhiannon is framed for murdering and eating him. She is sentenced to stand at the gates of the city for seven years, carrying visitors to the door of the castle on her back as though she herself were a horse.

Finally, their son reappears through an act of magic (which involves a mare and a foal), and Rhiannon returns to her position as Queen.

Often portrayed as a young woman wearing gold, surrounded by singing birds as she rides her white horse, Rhiannon also has a reputation as one who can bring dreams to those who seek the truth about a situation. Many Wiccans revere her for her lessons in patience, inner strength, and forgiveness, and especially casting aside the role of victim in many aspects of one's life.

Group rituals aimed at restoring social, economic, or environmental justice are definitely appropriate times to invoke her. You can also call on Rhiannon for assistance with fertility, self-confidence, inspiration, leadership, transformation, wisdom, divination, and improving magical skills in general.

If possible, it's ideal to honor Rhiannon in a grove or wooded area under moonlight. Of course, you can also dedicate an altar to her with symbols of the Moon, birds, horses and horseshoes, and the colors white and gold. Offerings of milk, hay, and sweetgrass are appreciated, along with soft music and white flowers.

CERNUNNOS

For all his popularity among Wiccans and other Pagans, not to mention the apparent widespread worship of him in the ancient Celtic world, very little is actually known about the god called Cernunnos. This may be due at least in part to the fact that the name "Cernunnos" is thought to come from a mix of Greco-Roman and Celtic languages, and so could actually be a newer, alternate name for a Celtic deity whose original identity remains unknown.

Images thought to be depictions of Cernunnos—a seated figure with the antlers of a stag on his head, often in the company of one or more animals—have been discovered throughout Western Europe. However, there is only one known artifact, a stone carving found in Paris, actually inscribed with this name.

Nonetheless, Cernunnos, whose name has been translated as "the horned," was an inspiration to the early Wiccans of the 20th century, and he is still seen by many today as the ultimate archetype on which to base the Wiccan God.

Cernunnos came to the attention of Gerald Gardner and other British occultists through the work of anthropologist Margaret Murray, who theorized that a pan-European, pre-Christian religion had worshipped a single Horned God who had different names in different parts of the world, and that Cernunnos was the name of the Horned God in Gaul. Murray also equated the English mythological figure Herne with this deity, which brought Cernunnos into even more direct connection to Gardner's revival of "the Old Religion."

Some contemporary scholars have made comparisons between Cernunnos and the Hindu god Shiva, while a few have made unproven claims that Cernunnos has an Irish equivalent called Uindos, who himself is equated with the hero Finn of Irish mythology.

Some of these theories have more evidence than others, but many worshippers of Cernunnos actually find the lack of concrete knowledge to be an advantage. The "blank slate" of Cernunnos can make it easier to adopt him into a modern pantheon—just as people in past millennia adopted deities from places and time periods other than their own.

In addition to the stag antlers, traditional images of Cernunnos portray him with one or more torcs—Celtic adornments signifying nobility—hanging from the antlers or around his neck. He is usually bearded and wild-haired, sitting in a cross-legged position, and often wearing a coin purse and holding a serpent. The serpent sometimes has the head, or at least the horns, of a ram.

Boars, bulls, and other powerful animals may be with him, and he may also hold a spear and shield. This imagery has led to his being called "Lord of the Animals," "Lord of the Hunt," and even Lord of Wild Things." Some worshippers see him as a shapeshifter, able to assume the form of any animal.

Wiccans have associated Cernunnos with virility, fertility, masculine energy and power, as the Celts likely did. Due to his association with forest animals, some equate him with the

Green Man. As such, he represents abundance and good fortune, but as a god of the hunt, he also has associations with death and dying.

Call on him for assistance with situations that require assertiveness and/or physical power. To honor Cernunnos, place images of antlers, horns, snakes, and/or forest animals on your altar, and offer musk, frankincense, and/or whole-grain bread.

WORKING WITH CELTIC DEITIES: A TABLE OF CORRESPONDENCES

Deity	Candle Colors	Images & Symbols	Offerings	Types of Magic
The Dagda	brown, green, gold	cauldron, oak tree, harp	hops, oak leaves	magical power, abundance, restoring order
Brighid	white, yellow, blue	flames, water, hearth, metal jewelry, dandelion, trillium	corn, oats, garden sage, pumpkin seeds	change, childbirth, communication, creativity, health/healing, new endeavors, opportunity
Lugh	yellow, gold, bronze	sun, harp, spear	bread, grains	knowledge, healing, building, creative skill
Rhiannon	gold, white	horse, moon, songbird, white flowers	milk, hay, sweetgrass	change, justice, health/healing, pets
Cernunnos	dark green, brown	antlers, snake, forest animals	musk, frankincense, whole-grain bread	magical power

CONCLUSION

The purpose of this guide is to provide you with a brief introduction to the Wiccan concepts of deity.

As we have seen, the Goddess and God, in their many forms, encompass the divine female and male energies of the Universe. Within this energy are countless deities who have existed since before the beginning of recorded history.

The paths to connection with the God and Goddess—or to any known ancient deities—are as multiple and varied as the people who worship them. If you see relationships with deities as a possible part of your path, by all means, continue exploring! Read about them—in Wiccan books, in history books, in ancient myths and poetry.

You'll find a few suggestions for getting started at the end of this guide. But also remember that it's just as important to listen to your intuition, and your heart, as this is what will ultimately guide you on your journey.

Thank you one more time for reading.

Blessed Be.

SUGGESTIONS FOR FURTHER READING

Please note that this is a very brief list. Many other interesting and useful resources about the pantheons covered in this guide, as well as the deities of the Norse, Hindu, African, Asian, and the Native American peoples are available in print and online.

Malcolm Day, *100 Characters from Classical Mythology: Discover the Fascinating Stories of the Greek and Roman Deities* (2007)

Janet and Stewart Farrar, *The Witches' God: Lord of the Dance* (1989)

Janet and Stewart Farrar, *The Witches' Goddess: The Feminine Principle of Divinity* (1987)

Felix Guirand, *New Larousse Encyclopedia of Mythology* (1987)

Sharon LaBorde, *Following the Sun: A Practical Guide to Egyptian Religion* (2010)

Edain McCoy, *Celtic Myth & Magick: Harness the Power of the Gods and Goddesses* (2002)

David Rankine, *The Isles of the Many Gods: An A-Z of the Pagan Gods and Goddesses Worshipped in Ancient Britain During the First Millennium Ce Through to the Middle Ages* (2007)

THREE FREE
AUDIOBOOKS PROMOTION

Don't forget, you can now enjoy **three audiobooks completely free of charge** when you start a free 30-day trial with Audible.

If you're new to the Craft, *Wicca Starter Kit* contains three of Lisa's most popular books for beginning Wiccans. You can download it for free at:

www.wiccaliving.com/free-wiccan-audiobooks

Or, if you're wanting to expand your magical skills, check out *Spellbook Starter Kit,* with three collections of spellwork featuring the powerful energies of candles, colors, crystals, mineral stones, and magical herbs. Download over 150 spells for free at:

www.wiccaliving.com/free-spell-audiobooks

Members receive free audiobooks every month, as well as exclusive discounts. And, if you don't want to continue with Audible, just remember to cancel your membership. You won't be charged a cent, and you'll get to keep your books!

Happy listening!

MORE BOOKS BY LISA CHAMBERLAIN

Wicca for Beginners: A Guide to Wiccan Beliefs, Rituals, Magic, and Witchcraft

Wicca Book of Spells: A Book of Shadows for Wiccans, Witches, and Other Practitioners of Magic

Wicca Herbal Magic: A Beginner's Guide to Practicing Wiccan Herbal Magic, with Simple Herb Spells

Wicca Book of Herbal Spells: A Book of Shadows for Wiccans, Witches, and Other Practitioners of Herbal Magic

Wicca Candle Magic: A Beginner's Guide to Practicing Wiccan Candle Magic, with Simple Candle Spells

Wicca Book of Candle Spells: A Book of Shadows for Wiccans, Witches, and Other Practitioners of Candle Magic

Wicca Crystal Magic: A Beginner's Guide to Practicing Wiccan Crystal Magic, with Simple Crystal Spells

Wicca Book of Crystal Spells: A Book of Shadows for Wiccans, Witches, and Other Practitioners of Crystal Magic

Tarot for Beginners: A Guide to Psychic Tarot Reading, Real Tarot Card Meanings, and Simple Tarot Spreads

Runes for Beginners: A Guide to Reading Runes in Divination, Rune Magic, and the Meaning of the Elder Futhark Runes

Wicca Moon Magic: A Wiccan's Guide and Grimoire for Working Magic with Lunar Energies

Wicca Wheel of the Year Magic: A Beginner's Guide to the Sabbats, with History, Symbolism, Celebration Ideas, and Dedicated Sabbat Spells

Wicca Kitchen Witchery: A Beginner's Guide to Magical Cooking, with Simple Spells and Recipes

Wicca Essential Oils Magic: A Beginner's Guide to Working with Magical Oils, with Simple Recipes and Spells

Wicca Elemental Magic: A Guide to the Elements, Witchcraft, and Magical Spells

Wicca Magical Deities: A Guide to the Wiccan God and Goddess, and Choosing a Deity to Work Magic With

Wicca Living a Magical Life: A Guide to Initiation and Navigating Your Journey in the Craft

Magic and the Law of Attraction: A Witch's Guide to the Magic of Intention, Raising Your Frequency, and Building Your Reality

Wicca Altar and Tools: A Beginner's Guide to Wiccan Altars, Tools for Spellwork, and Casting the Circle

Wicca Finding Your Path: A Beginner's Guide to Wiccan Traditions, Solitary Practitioners, Eclectic Witches, Covens, and Circles

Wicca Book of Shadows: A Beginner's Guide to Keeping Your Own Book of Shadows and the History of Grimoires

Modern Witchcraft and Magic for Beginners: A Guide to Traditional and Contemporary Paths, with Magical Techniques for the Beginner Witch

FREE GIFT REMINDER

Just a reminder that Lisa is giving away an exclusive, free spell book as a thank-you gift to new readers!

Little Book of Spells contains ten spells that are ideal for newcomers to the practice of magic, but are also suitable for any level of experience.

Read it on read on your laptop, phone, tablet, Kindle or Nook device by visiting:

www.wiccaliving.com/bonus

DID YOU ENJOY
WICCA MAGICAL DEITIES?

Thanks so much for reading this book! I know there are many great books out there about Wicca, so I really appreciate you choosing this one.

If you enjoyed the book, I have a small favor to ask—would you take a couple of minutes to leave a review for this book on Amazon?

Your feedback will help me to make improvements to this book, and to create even better ones in the future. It will also help me develop new ideas for books on other topics that might be of interest to you. Thanks in advance for your help!

CPSIA information can be obtained
at www.ICGtesting.com
Printed in the USA
LVHW020508160321
681656LV00012B/207